Kaplan Publishing are constantly finding new ways to make a difference to your studies and our exciting online resources r̶ ̶ ̶ ̶ ̶ ̶ thing different to students lookir̶ ̶ ̶ ̶.

D1386207

This book comes with free MyKaplan online resources so that you can study anytime, anywhere. **This free online resource is not sold separately and is included in the price of the book.**

Having purchased this book, you have access to the following online study materials:

CONTENT	AAT	
	Text	Kit
Electronic version of the book	✓	✓
Progress tests with instant answers	✓	
Mock assessments online	✓	✓
Material updates	✓	✓

How to access your online resources

Kaplan Financial students will already have a MyKaplan account and these extra resources will be available to you online. You do not need to register again, as this process was completed when you enrolled. If you are having problems accessing online materials, please ask your course administrator.

If you are not studying with Kaplan and did not purchase your book via a Kaplan website, to unlock your extra online resources please go to www.mykaplan.co.uk/addabook (even if you have set up an account and registered books previously). You will then need to enter the ISBN number (on the title page and back cover) and the unique pass key number contained in the scratch panel below to gain access. You will also be required to enter additional information during this process to set up or confirm your account details.

If you purchased through Kaplan Flexible Learning or via the Kaplan Publishing website you will automatically receive an e-mail invitation to MyKaplan. Please register your details using this email to gain access to your content. If you do not receive the e-mail or book content, please contact Kaplan Publishing.

Your Code and Information

This code can only be used once for the registration of one book online. This registration and your online content will expire when the final sittings for the examinations covered by this book have taken place. Please allow one hour from the time you submit your book details for us to process your request.

Please scratch the film to access your MyKaplan code.

Please be aware that this code is case-sensitive and you will need to include the dashes within the passcode, but not when entering the ISBN. For further technical support, please visit www.MyKaplan.co.uk

AAT

AQ2016

Management Accounting: Costing

EXAM KIT

This Exam Kit supports study for the following AAT qualifications:

AAT Advanced Diploma in Accounting – Level 3

AAT Advanced Certificate in Bookkeeping – Level 3

AAT Advanced Diploma in Accounting at SCQF Level 6

PUBLISHING

British Library Cataloguing-in-Publication Data

A catalogue record for this book is available from the British Library.

Published by:

Kaplan Publishing UK

Unit 2 The Business Centre

Molly Millar's Lane

Wokingham

Berkshire

RG41 2QZ

ISBN: 978-1-78740-530-1

© Kaplan Financial Limited, 2019

Printed and bound in Great Britain

CONTENTS

Features in this revision kit

In addition to providing a wide ranging bank of real exam style questions, we have also included in this kit:

- unit specific information and advice on exam technique

- our recommended approach to make your revision for this particular subject as effective as possible.

You will find a wealth of other resources to help you with your studies on the AAT website:

www.aat.org.uk/

Quality and accuracy are of the utmost importance to us so if you spot an error in any of our products, please send an email to mykaplanreporting@kaplan.com with full details, or follow the link to the feedback form in MyKaplan.

Our Quality Co-ordinator will work with our technical team to verify the error and take action to ensure it is corrected in future editions.

UNIT SPECIFIC INFORMATION

THE EXAM

FORMAT OF THE ASSESSMENT

The assessment will comprise ten independent tasks. Students will normally be assessed by computer-based assessment.

In any one assessment, students may not be assessed on all content, or on the full depth or breadth of a piece of content. The content assessed may change over time to ensure validity of assessment, but all assessment criteria will be tested over time.

The learning outcomes for this unit are as follows:

	Learning outcome	Weighting
1	Understanding the purpose and use of management accounting within an organisation	15%
2	Apply techniques required for dealing with costs	35%
3	Apportion costs according to organisational requirements	19%
4	Analyse and review deviations from budget and report these to management	10%
5	Apply management accounting techniques to support decision making	21%
	Total	100%

Time allowed

2 ½ hours

PASS MARK

The pass mark for all AAT CBAs is 70%.

 Always keep your eye on the clock and make sure you attempt all questions!

DETAILED SYLLABUS

The detailed syllabus and study guide written by the AAT can be found at:

www.aat.org.uk/

INDEX TO QUESTIONS AND ANSWERS

EXAM TECHNIQUE

- **Do not skip any of the material** in the syllabus.

- **Read each question** *very* carefully.

- **Double-check your answer** before committing yourself to it.

- Answer **every** question – if you do not know an answer to a multiple choice question or true/false question, you don't lose anything by guessing. Think carefully before you **guess**.

- If you are answering a multiple-choice question, **eliminate first those answers that you know are wrong**. Then choose the most appropriate answer from those that are left.

- **Don't panic** if you realise you've answered a question incorrectly. Getting one question wrong will not mean the difference between passing and failing

Computer-based exams – tips

- Do not attempt a CBA until you have **completed all study material** relating to it.

- On the AAT website there is a CBA demonstration. It is **ESSENTIAL** that you attempt this before your real CBA. You will become familiar with how to move around the CBA screens and the way that questions are formatted, increasing your confidence and speed in the actual exam.

- Be sure you understand how to use the **software** before you start the exam. If in doubt, ask the assessment centre staff to explain it to you.

- Questions are **displayed on the screen** and answers are entered using keyboard and mouse. At the end of the exam, you are given a certificate showing the result you have achieved.

- In addition to the traditional multiple-choice question type, CBAs will also contain **other types of questions**, such as number entry questions, drag and drop, true/false, pick lists or drop down menus or hybrids of these.

- You need to be sure you **know how to answer questions** of this type before you sit the exam, through practice.

KAPLAN'S RECOMMENDED REVISION APPROACH

QUESTION PRACTICE IS THE KEY TO SUCCESS

Success in professional examinations relies upon you acquiring a firm grasp of the required knowledge at the tuition phase. In order to be able to do the questions, knowledge is essential.

However, the difference between success and failure often hinges on your exam technique on the day and making the most of the revision phase of your studies.

The **Kaplan textbook** is the starting point, designed to provide the underpinning knowledge to tackle all questions. However, in the revision phase, poring over text books is not the answer.

Kaplan pocket notes are designed to help you quickly revise a topic area; however you then need to practise questions. There is a need to progress to exam style questions as soon as possible, and to tie your exam technique and technical knowledge together.

The importance of question practice cannot be over-emphasised.

The recommended approach below is designed by expert tutors in the field, in conjunction with their knowledge of the examiner and the specimen assessment.

You need to practise as many questions as possible in the time you have left.

OUR AIM

Our aim is to get you to the stage where you can attempt exam questions confidently, to time, in a closed book environment, with no supplementary help (i.e. to simulate the real examination experience).

Practising your exam technique is also vitally important for you to assess your progress and identify areas of weakness that may need more attention in the final run up to the examination.

In order to achieve this we recognise that initially you may feel the need to practice some questions with open book help.

Good exam technique is vital.

THE KAPLAN REVISION PLAN

Stage 1: Assess areas of strengths and weaknesses

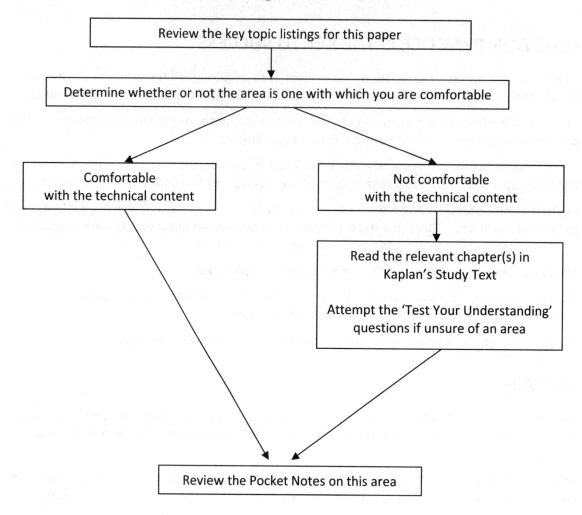

Review the key topic listings for this paper

Determine whether or not the area is one with which you are comfortable

Comfortable
with the technical content

Not comfortable
with the technical content

Read the relevant chapter(s) in
Kaplan's Study Text

Attempt the 'Test Your Understanding'
questions if unsure of an area

Review the Pocket Notes on this area

Stage 2: Practise questions

Follow the order of revision of topics as presented in this kit and attempt the questions in the order suggested.

Try to avoid referring to text books and notes and the model answer until you have completed your attempt.

Review your attempt with the model answer and assess how much of the answer you achieved.

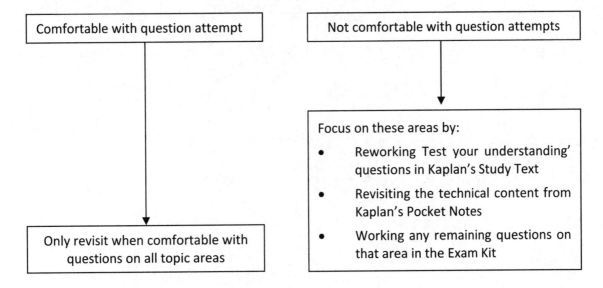

Comfortable with question attempt

Not comfortable with question attempts

Only revisit when comfortable with questions on all topic areas

Focus on these areas by:

- Reworking Test your understanding' questions in Kaplan's Study Text
- Revisiting the technical content from Kaplan's Pocket Notes
- Working any remaining questions on that area in the Exam Kit

Stage 3: Final pre-exam revision

We recommend that you **attempt at least one two and a half hour mock examination** containing a set of previously unseen exam standard questions.

Attempt the mock CBA online in timed, closed book conditions to simulate the real exam experience

Section 1

PRACTICE QUESTIONS

INVENTORY

INVENTORY

1   Which of the following is least relevant to the simple economic order quantity model for inventory?

   A   Safety inventory

   B   Annual demand

   C   Holding costs

   D   Ordering costs

2   The EOQ formula includes the cost of placing an order. However, the management accountant is unsure which of the following items would usually be included in 'cost of placing an order'

   (i)   administrative costs

   (ii)   postage

   (iii) quality control costs

   (iv)   unit cost of products

   (v)   storekeeper's salary

   Which three of the above would be regarded as part of the cost of placing an order?

   A   (i), (ii) and (iii)

   B   (i), (iv) and (v)

   C   (ii), (iii) and (iv)

   D   (i), (ii) and (v)

3   A business, which orders 500 units each time, has looked at the delivery time and usage for the raw material and it has the following data:

   Usage: between 500 and 800 a week

   Lead time: between 1 and 3 weeks

   •   **Calculate the maximum inventory level**

   •   **Calculate the minimum inventory level**

4 PLASTIC

The following information is available for plastic grade PM7:

- Annual demand 112,500 kilograms.
- Annual holding cost per kilogram £1.80
- Fixed ordering cost £3.60

(a) Calculate the Economic Order Quantity (EOQ) for PM7 (round to the nearest whole number)

The inventory record shown below for plastic grade PM7 for the month of July has only been fully completed for the first three weeks of the month.

(b) Complete the entries in the inventory record for the two receipts on 24 and 28 July that were ordered using the EOQ method.

(c) Complete ALL entries in the inventory record for the two issues in the month and for the closing balance at the end of July using the FIFO method of issuing inventory.

(Show the costs per kilogram (kg) in £'s to 3 decimal places; and the total costs in whole £'s).

Inventory record for plastic grade PM7

Date	Receipts Quantity kgs	Receipts Cost per kg (£)	Receipts Total cost (£)	Issues Quantity kgs	Issues Cost per kg (£)	Issues Total cost (£)	Balance Quantity kgs	Balance Total cost (£)
Balance as at 22 July							198	238
24 July		2.336						
26 July				540				
28 July		2.344						
30 July				710				

(d) Using the LIFO method, the issue of 540 kg to production on the 26 July would be valued at a total of (to the nearest whole number)_____.

5   SURESTICK GLUE

The following information is available for direct material SURESTICK GLUE:

- Fixed ordering cost £2.50
- Annual holding cost per litre £1.00
- Monthly demand 2,500 litres

(a)   Calculate the Economic Order Quantity (EOQ) for direct material SURESTICK GLUE (round your answer up to the nearest whole number)

The inventory record shown below for SURESTICK GLUE for the month of June has only been fully completed for the first three weeks of the month.

(b)   Complete the entries in the inventory record for the two receipts on 24 and 27 June that were ordered using the EOQ method.

(c)   Complete ALL entries in the inventory record for the two issues in the month and for the closing balance at the end of June using the AVCO method of issuing inventory.

(Show the costs per litre in £'s to 3 decimal places; and the total costs in whole £'s, round up to nearest whole number).

Inventory record for SURESTICK GLUE

Date	Receipts			Issues			Balance	
	Quantity litres	Cost per litre (£)	Total cost (£)	Quantity litres	Cost per litre (£)	Total cost (£)	Quantity litres	Total cost (£)
Balance as at 23 June							65	130
24 June		2.234						
26 June				180				
27 June		2.341						
30 June				250				

(d)   Using the LIFO method, the issue of 180 kg to production on the 26 June would be valued at a total of _____ .

6   GRAPE LTD

The inventory record shown below for glaze for the month of January has only been fully completed for the first three weeks of the month.

(a)   Identify the inventory valuation method used to complete the inventory record:

    A   FIFO

    B   LIFO

    C   AVCO

(b)   Complete ALL entries in the inventory record for the two issues in the month and identified in part (a)

(Show the costs per drum in £'s to 3 decimal places; and the total costs in whole £'s).

Inventory record for glaze

Date	Receipts Quantity drums	Receipts Cost per drum (£)	Receipts Total cost (£)	Issues Quantity drums	Issues Cost per drum (£)	Issues Total cost (£)	Balance Quantity drums	Balance Total cost (£)
Balance as at 22 January							1,650	1,980
25 January	1,200	1.250					2,850	3,480
26 January				1,300		1,587		
28 January	1,200	1.302						
31 January				1,500				

(c)   Complete the following sentence with regard to LIFO as a method of pricing inventory

The LIFO method for costing issues **will/will not*** always mean that inventory is physically issued on a rotating basis so that the last inventory in is the first inventory issued.

7   GLOBE LTD

(a)   Identify the inventory valuation method used to complete the inventory record:

   A   FIFO

   B   LIFO

   C   AVCO

(b)   Complete ALL entries in the inventory record for the two issues in the month and for the closing balance at the end of March using the method of issuing inventory identified in part (a)

   (Show the costs per tonne in £'s to 2 decimal places; and the total costs in whole £'s).

Inventory record for M2

Date	Receipts			Issues			Balance	
	Quantity tonnes	Cost per tonne (£)	Total cost (£)	Quantity tonnes	Cost per tonne (£)	Total cost (£)	Quantity tonnes	Total cost (£)
Balance as at 27 March							1,200	14,400
28 March	800	12.50					2,000	24,400
29 March				820		9,840		
30 March	800	12.25						
31 March				900				

8   In a period of rising prices, which type of inventory valuation shows the highest profit?

   A   FIFO

   B   LIFO

   C   AVCO

   D   None

9   In times of rising prices, the valuation of inventory using the First In First Out method, as opposed to the Weighted Average Cost method, will result in which ONE of the following combinations?

	Cost of sales	Profit	Closing inventory
A	Lower	Higher	Higher
B	Lower	Higher	Lower
C	Higher	Lower	Higher
D	Higher	Higher	Lower

10   JUMP LTD

Jump Ltd had the following inventory of wooden poles:

Date purchased	Quantity	Cost per pole (£)	Total cost (£)
May 6	50	8.00	400
May 13	80	7.50	600
May 20	60	7.00	420

Jump Ltd issued 70 poles on the 25th May

(a)   **Calculate the value of the issue and the balance after the issue using AVCO, FIFO and LIFO (round to 4 decimal places for the cost per unit and round to the nearest pound for the final answer):**

	Cost £
AVCO issue	
FIFO issue	
LIFO issue	
AVCO balance	
FIFO balance	
LIFO balance	

(b)   **Which of the following costs would NEVER be included in Jump Ltd's inventory valuation?**

A   Prime costs

B   Product costs

C   Marginal costs

D   Period costs

JOURNAL ENTRIES

INVENTORY

11 The following represent the materials transactions for a company for the month of December 20X6:

	£000s
Materials purchases	176
Issued to production	165
Materials written off	4
Returned to stores	9
Returned to suppliers	8

The material inventory at 1 December 20X6 was £15,000.

What is the closing balance on the materials inventory account at 31 December 20X6?

A   £5,000

B   £16,000

C   £23,000

D   £31,000

12 A number of transactions took place during October that need to be entered into the cost accounting records of Truck Transport Ltd.

The follow cost accounting codes are used:

Code	Description
2000	Bank
3000	PLCA
4000	Stores
5000	Maintenance
6000	General administration
8000	Direct costs
9000	Indirect costs

Identify the correct cost accounting entry for each of the following FOUR accounting transactions:

(a)   **Return of 20 flap straps, costed at £50 each, from Maintenance to Stores**

	Code	£
Debit		
Credit		

(b) Payment to supplier for 15 padded steering wheels. These cost £75 each and were purchased on 30 day credit terms

	Code	£
Debit		
Credit		

(c) Payment on receipt of a delivery of fuel costing £1,200

	Code	£
Debit		
Credit		

(d) Issue of 300 litres of fuel at £1.23 to the short haul department

	Code	£
Debit		
Credit		

13 The double entry for an issue of indirect production materials would be:

A Dr Materials control account Cr Finished goods control account

B Dr Production overhead control a/c Cr Materials control account

C Dr Work-in-progress control account Cr Production overhead control a/c

D Dr Work-in-progress control account Cr Materials control account

LABOUR

14 Below are extracts from Jump Ltd's payroll for last week

Date	Labour cost
6 May	Stores department Employees pay £1,500 + 10% bonus
11 May	Administration department Staff salaries £5,000 + 15% bonus
13 May	Wood trimming Production employees pay 600 hours at £8.50 per hour
15 May	Wood painting Production employees basic pay £5,500 + £300 overtime

The cost codes for the different accounts are:

Non-operating overheads	6000
Operating overheads	5000
Wages control account	4000
Wood painting direct costs	3021
Wood trimming direct costs	3022

Complete the cost journal entries to record the four payroll payments made in May

Date	Code	Dr £	Cr £
6 May			
6 May			
11 May			
11 May			
13 May			
13 May			
15 May			
15 May			

15 The payroll for maintenance employees for the week ending 30 November has been completed. The following payments are to be made:

	£
Net wages/salaries to pay to employees	10,000
Income tax and national insurance contributions (NIC) to pay to HMRC	2,000
Pension contributions to pay to F4L pension scheme	1,000
	_____
Gross payroll costs	13,000

The payroll for the week is analysed as:

	£
Direct labour costs	7,000
Indirect labour costs	4,000
Maintenance administration labour costs	2,000
	_____
Gross payroll costs	13,000

The following cost account codes are used to record maintenance labour costs:

Code	Description
6200	Maintenance direct labour
6400	Maintenance overheads
6600	Maintenance administration
8200	Wages control

(a) **Complete the wages control account entries in the account shown below:**

Wages control account			
	£		£
Bank (net wages/salaries)		Maintenance (direct labour)	
HMRC (income tax and NIC)		Maintenance overheads	
Pension contributions		Maintenance administration	
	13,000		13,000

(b) **Complete the table below to show how the gross payroll cost for the week is charged to the various cost accounts of the business:**

Date	Code	Debit	Credit
30 November			
30 November			
30 November			
30 November			
30 November			
30 November			

16 A number of transactions took place during October that need to be entered into the cost accounting records of Truck Transport Ltd.

The follow cost accounting codes are used:

Code   **Description**
1000   Bank
4000   PLCA
5000   Stores
6000   Wages Control
7000   General administration
8000   Direct costs
9000   Indirect costs

Identify the correct cost accounting entry for each of the following FOUR accounting transactions:

(a) **Payment of driver wages for the week amounting to 490 hours at £15.50 per hour**

	Code	£
Debit		
Credit		

(b) Drivers worked 20 hours of overtime at time and a half at the specific request of a customer. How would the overtime premium be recorded in the accounts?

	Code	£
Debit		
Credit		

(c) The stores supervisor monthly salary of £2,000

	Code	£
Debit		
Credit		

(d) Drivers worked 10 hours of overtime at time and a half due to general work pressures. How would the overtime premium be recorded in the accounts?

	Code	£
Debit		
Credit		

OVERHEADS

17 At the end of a period, in an integrated cost and financial accounting system, the accounting entries for £10,000 overheads over-absorbed would be:

A	Dr	Work-in-progress control account	Cr	Overhead control account
B	Dr	Statement of profit or loss	Cr	Work-in-progress control account
C	Dr	Statement of profit or loss	Cr	Overhead control account
D	Dr	Overhead control account	Cr	Statement of profit or loss

18 During a period £50,000 was incurred for indirect labour. In a typical cost ledger, the double entry for this is:

A	Dr	Wages control	Cr	Overhead control
B	Dr	WIP control	Cr	Wages control
C	Dr	Overhead control	Cr	Wages control
D	Dr	Wages control	Cr	WIP control

LABOUR COSTS

LABOUR

19   CARTCYLE LTD

Below is a weekly timesheet for one of Cartcyle Ltd's employees, who are paid as follows:

- For a basic six-hour shift every day from Monday to Friday – basic pay.

- For any overtime in excess of the basic six hours, on any day from Monday to Friday – the extra hours are paid at time-and-a-half (basic pay plus an overtime premium equal to half of basic pay).

- For three contracted hours each Saturday morning – basic pay.

- For any hours in excess of three hours on Saturday – the extra hours are paid at double time (basic pay plus an overtime premium equal to basic pay).

- For any hours worked on Sunday – paid at double time (basic pay plus an overtime premium equal to basic pay).

Complete the columns headed Basic pay, Overtime premium and Total pay:

(**Notes:** Zero figures should be entered in cells where appropriate)

Employee's weekly timesheet for week ending 7 December

Employee:		A.Man		Profit centre:			Wood finishing	
Employee number:		C812		Basic pay per hour:			£8.00	
	Hours spent on production	Hours worked on indirect work	Notes		Basic pay £	Overtime premium £		Total pay £
Monday	6	2	10am – 12am cleaning of machinery					
Tuesday	2	4	9am – 1pm customer care course					
Wednesday	8							
Thursday	6							
Friday	6	1	3 – 4pm health and safety training					
Saturday	6							
Sunday	3							
Total	**37**	**7**						

20 A company employs a group of production workers who, as well as earning basic pay, are also paid a weekly group bonus based on their productivity during each week.

The group has a standard (target) output of 800 units of production per hour worked. All output in excess of this level earns a bonus for each of the employees.

The bonus % is calculated as:

$$25\% \times \frac{\text{Excess production (units)}}{\text{Standard production (units)}} \times 100$$

The bonus rate per hour is then calculated as: bonus % × £10.

The following information relates to this group's performance last week:

	Hours worked	Actual production (units)
Monday	920	940,000
Tuesday	870	890,000
Wednesday	910	930,000
Thursday	920	960,000
Friday	940	990,000
Saturday	440	690,000
Total	5,000	5,400,000

(a) **Use the table below to calculate the group bonus rate per hour and the total bonus to be paid to the group.**

	Units
Actual production	
Less standard production (based on actual hours worked)	
Excess production	
Bonus %	
Group bonus rate per hour £	
Total group bonus £	

(b) **An employee in this group worked for 44 hours last week, and is paid a basic rate of £9.60 per hour. The employee's total pay for last week was:**

£ ☐

21 GRAPES

Below is a weekly timesheet for one of Grape's employees, who are paid as follows:

- For a basic seven-hour shift every day from Monday to Friday – basic pay.

- For any overtime in excess of the basic seven hours, on any day from Monday to Friday – the extra hours are paid at basic pay plus an overtime premium is added of 50% of basic pay.

- For two contracted hours each Saturday morning – basic pay.

- For any hours in excess of two hours on Saturday – the overtime premium is paid at 75% of basic pay.

Complete the columns headed Basic pay, Overtime premium and Total pay:

(Notes: Zero figures should be entered in cells where appropriate)

Employee's weekly timesheet for week ending 31 January

Employee:		Olivia Michael	Profit centre:		Moulding Department	
Employee number:	P450		**Basic pay per hour:**	£10.00		
	Hours spent in work	Hours spent on indirect work	Notes	Basic pay £	Overtime premium £	Total pay £
Monday	8	3	10am – 1pm cleaning moulds			
Tuesday	7	4	9am – 1pm fire training			
Wednesday	8					
Thursday	7	1				
Friday	7	1	3 – 4pm annual appraisal			
Saturday	3					
Total	**40**	**9**				

Analyse the timesheet into production cost and production overhead costs.

Labour cost account

	£		£
Bank		Production	
		Production overheads	

22   Truck Transport Ltd employs a team of four mechanics who regularly service and valet the trucks.

The mechanics are paid a basic rate of £15.00 per hour and any overtime is paid at the following rates:

- Overtime rate 1: basic pay + 30%

- Overtime rate 2: basic pay + 50%

Truck transport sets a target for mechanics each month. A bonus equal to 75% of the basic hourly rate is payable for every service or valet in excess of the target.

The target for June for servicing was 50 trucks and 60 valets. The team completed 55 services and 63 valets.

All driving instructors work the same number of hours. Overtime premiums and bonuses are included as part of the indirect labour cost.

(a)   **Complete the gaps in the table below to calculate the total labour cost for the mechanics.**

Labour cost	Hours	£
Basic pay	620	
Overtime rate 1	36	
Overtime rate 2	20	
Total cost before bonus		
Bonus payment		
Total cost including bonus		

(b)   **Calculate the direct labour cost per mechanic for June**

£

(c)   **Complete the following sentence.**

The total pay, including bonus, for each mechanic for June (to TWO decimal places) was:

£

and of this total, the bonus payable to each team member (to TWO decimal places) was:

£

23 A company operates a piecework system of remuneration. Employees must work for a minimum of 37 hours per week. Sebastian produces the following output for a particular week:

Product	Quantity	Standard time per item (hours)	Total actual time (hours)
Buckles	50	0.2	9
Press studs	200	0.06	14
Belts	100	0.1	12
Buttons	10	0.7	6
			41

Sebastian is paid £8.00 per standard hour worked. What are his earnings for the week?

A £296

B £302

C £312

D £328

24 Employees work in a team of 5 in the Wood painting department of Jump Ltd. They are paid a basic rate of £15 per hour, and any overtime is paid at the following rates:

- Overtime rate 1 – basic pay + 50%

- Overtime rate 2 – double pay

There is a target for painting wood each month and bonus of 10% of the basic hourly rate is paid for each pole painted in excess of the target.

The target for May was 3,000 poles and the team managed to paint 3,500 poles.

All the team members work the same number of hours and all overtime and bonuses are included as part of the direct labour cost.

(a) **Complete the gaps in the table below to calculate the total labour cost for the team in May**

Labour cost	Hours	£	Working
Basic pay	500		
Overtime rate 1	50		
Overtime rate 2	20		
Total cost before bonus	570		
Bonus			
Total cost including bonus			

(b)   **Calculate the total labour cost of painting a pole in May:**

(c)   **Complete the following sentences:**

The basic pay and overtime for each member of the team in May was £

The bonus payable to each team member was £

25   Information is available relating to the production of the tins of cat food for the month of July:

Total number of labour hours worked	10,800
Overtime hours worked	2,450
Standard hours for production in July	11,200
Normal rate per hour	£9
Overtime payment per hour	£14.50

The company operates a group incentive scheme, whereby a bonus of 35% of the normal hourly rate is paid for hours saved.

(a)   **Calculate the total cost of direct labour for July, assuming that overtime and the bonus are due to a specific customer request.**

Total basic pay (£)	
Total overtime premium (£)	
Hours saved (hours)	
Bonus (£)	
Total direct labour cost (£)	

(b)   In August the bonus was based on equivalent units. Employees will receive 45% of the basic hourly rate for every equivalent unit in excess of target. Rates of pay are not due to change in August. The target production is 450 units.

At the end of August 300 units were completed and there were 200 units of closing work in progress that was 100% complete for material and 75% complete for labour.

Calculate the number of equivalent units with regards to labour and the bonus payable

Equivalent units	
Bonus (£)	

ACCOUNTING FOR OVERHEADS

OVERHEAD ALLOCATION AND APPORTIONMENT

26   What is cost apportionment?

A   The charging of discrete identifiable items of cost to cost centres or cost units

B   The collection of costs attributable to cost centres and cost units using the costing methods, principles and techniques prescribed for a particular business entity

C   The process of establishing the costs of cost centres or cost units

D   The division of costs amongst two or more cost centres in proportion to the estimated benefit received, using a proxy, e.g. square feet

27   CARTCYLE LTD

Cartcyle Ltd's budgeted overheads for the next financial year are:

	£	£
Depreciation of plant and equipment		1,447,470
Power for production machinery		1,287,000
Rent and rates		188,100
Light and heat		41,580
Indirect labour costs:		
Maintenance	182,070	
Stores	64,890	
Administration	432,180	
Total indirect labour cost		679,140

The following information is also available:

Department	Carrying value of plant and equipment	Production machinery power usage (KwH)	Floor space (square metres)	Number of employees
Production:				
Wood cutting	10,080,000	3,861,000		25
Wood finishing	4,320,000	2,574,000		18
Support:				
Maintenance			25,200	9
Stores			15,120	3
Administration			10,080	12
Total	14,400,000	6,435,000	50,400	67

Overheads are allocated or apportioned on the most appropriate basis. The total overheads of the support cost centres are then reapportioned to the two production centres using the direct method.

- 70% of the Maintenance cost centre's time is spent maintaining production machinery in the Wood cutting production centre and the remainder in the Wood finishing production centre.

- The Stores cost centre makes 65% of its issues to the Wood cutting production centre, and 35% to the Wood finishing production centre.

- Administration supports the two production centres equally.

There is no reciprocal servicing between the three support cost centres.

Complete the overhead analysis table below:

	Basis of apportionment	Wood cutting £	Wood Finishing £	Maintenance £	Stores £	Admin £	Totals £
Depreciation of plant and equipment							
Power for production machinery							
Rent and rates							
Light and heat							
Indirect labour							
Totals							
Reapportion Maintenance							
Reapportion Stores							
Reapportion Admin.							
Total overheads to production centres							

28   AQUARIUS

Aquarius Ltd calculates depreciation on a reducing balance basis, and allocates and apportions other overheads using the most appropriate basis for each

(a)   Complete the table below to identify a suitable basis for allocating or apportioning each overhead by selecting the most appropriate option.

Overhead	Basis
Depreciation of plant and equipment	
Power for production machinery	
Rent and rates	
Light and heat	

Options:

- Carrying value of plant and equipment
- Production machinery power usage
- Floor space
- Indirect labour hours
- Number of employees

Aquarius has already allocated and apportioned its current costs for the next quarter, as shown in the table below. These costs have yet to be reapportioned to the two cost centres Assembly and Finishing.

The overhead allocated and apportioned to Administration is re-apportioned to the other production and support cost centres based on the number of employees. The number of employees is each department is:

Assembly 10, Finishing 10, Maintenance 6, Stores 4, Administration 8

The Stores cost centre makes 50% of its issues to the Assembly production centre, 30% to the Finishing production centre and 20% to Maintenance.

75% of the Maintenance cost centre's time is spent maintaining production machinery in the Assembly production centre and the remainder in the Finishing production centre.

(b) **Complete the table by reapportioning costs on the basis of the information given above. Enter your answers in whole pounds only. Indicate negative figures with minus signs, NOT brackets.**

	Assembly £	Finishing £	Maintenance £	Stores £	Admin £	Totals £
Depreciation of plant and equipment	420,000	280,000	–	–	–	700,000
Power for production machinery	403,000	217,000	–	–	–	620,000
Rent and rates	–	–	48,000	32,000	20,000	100,000
Light and heat	–	–	9,600	6,400	4,000	20,000
Indirect labour	–	–	102,000	40,000	240,000	382,000
Totals	**823,000**	**497,000**	**159,600**	**78,400**	**264,000**	**1,822,000**
Reapportion Admin						
Reapportion Stores						
Reapportion Maintenance						
Total overheads to production centres						

Another overhead is quality control costs. The estimated cost for the next quarter is £150,000, which consists of a fixed element and a variable element. The fixed element is 35% of the total cost and the rest is variable. The fixed element of the total cost is to be apportioned between the Assembly and Finishing departments in a ratio of 47:53. The variable element of the cost is apportioned in the ratio of 38:62.

(c) **Complete the following sentences by inserting the correct values.**

The fixed element of the quality control costs that will be apportioned to the Assembly department is:

£

The variable element of the quality control costs that will be apportioned to the Finishing department is:

£

29 F4L

F4L has budgeted for the following overheads for its two profit and three cost centres for quarter 1 of the next financial year:

	£000	£000
Depreciation of aircraft		36,400
Aviation fuel and other variable costs		42,200
Pilots and aircrew salaries:		
Scheduled services	5,250	
Charter flights	4,709	
Total pilots and aircrew salaries		9,959
Rent and rates and other premises costs		12,600
Indirect labour costs:		
Aircraft maintenance and repairs	9,600	
Fuel and parts store	3,200	
General administration	7,800	
Total indirect labour cost		20,600

The following information is also available:

Profit/cost centre	Carrying amount of aircraft (£000)	Planned number of miles flown	Floor space (square metres)	Number of employees
Scheduled services	1,080,000	215,600		105
Charter flights	720,000	176,400		96
Aircraft maintenance and repairs			190,000	260
Fuel and parts store			114,000	146
General administration			76,000	220
Total	1,800,000	392,000	380,000	827

Primary allocations or apportionments are made on the most appropriate basis. The support cost centres are then reapportioned to the two flight profit centres using the direct method.

- The Aircraft maintenance and repairs cost centre spends 60% of its time maintaining the aircraft in the scheduled services profit centre and the remainder in the charter flights profit centre.

- 55% of the issues from the Fuel and parts store cost centre are made to the scheduled services profit centre and the remainder to the charter flights profit centre.

- The scheduled services profit centre and the charter flights profit centre both incur general administration costs equally.

- The three support cost centres are not involved in reciprocal servicing.

Use the following table to allocate or apportion the overheads between the profit/cost centres, using the most appropriate basis.

	Basis of apportionment	Scheduled services £000	Charter flights £000	Aircraft maintenance and repairs £000	Fuel and parts store £000	General admin. £000	Totals £000
Depreciation of aircraft							
Aviation fuel and other variable costs							
Pilots and aircrew salaries							
Rent and rates and other premises costs							
Indirect labour							
Totals							
Reapportion Aircraft maintenance and repairs							
Reapportion Fuel and parts store							
Reapportion General admin.							
Total overheads to profit centres							

30   PREMIER LABELS LTD

Premier Labels Ltd produces labelled plastic food containers. The budgeted overheads for the next quarter are shown below, together with their behaviour and how they are apportioned to departments.

Budgeted cost	Cost behaviour	£	Comments
Heat and lighting	Semi-variable	60,000	Apportion fixed element of £24,000 equally between all four departments. Apportion variable element according to floor area.
Power for machinery	Variable	28,000	Apportion 70% to Plastics Moulding, and 30% to Labelling.
Supervision	Fixed	120,000	Apportion to the two production departments pro rata to direct labour costs.
Stores wages	Fixed	72,000	
Equipment Maintenance salaries	Fixed	188,200	
Depreciation of non-current assets	Fixed	84,000	Apportion according to carrying value of non-current assets.
Other overhead costs	Dependant on specific cost	128,000	Apportion 60% to Plastics Moulding, 20% to Labelling, and 10% each to Stores and Equipment Maintenance.

The following information is also available:

Department	Square metres occupied	Carrying value of non-current assets (£)	Number of material requisitions	Direct labour costs (£)
Plastics Moulding	320,000	160,000	162,750	100,000
Labelling	180,000	80,000	56,000	140,000
Stores	80,000	30,000		
Equipment Maintenance	20,000	10,000		

Notes: The Equipment Maintenance department's total costs should be apportioned equally to the other three departments. Then the total of the Stores department's costs should be apportioned according to the number of material requisitions.

Complete the overhead analysis table below:

	Basis of apportionment	Plastics Moulding	Labelling	Stores	Equipment Maintenance	Totals
Heat and lighting fixed cost						
Heat and lighting variable cost						
Power for machinery						
Supervision						
Stores wages						
Equipment maintenance salaries						
Depreciation of non-current assets						
Other overhead costs						
Totals						
Reapportion Equipment maintenance						
Reapportion stores						
Total overheads to profit centres						

KAPLAN PUBLISHING

OVERHEAD ABSORPTION

31 **An overhead absorption rate is used to:**

A   share out common costs over benefiting cost centres

B   find the total overheads for a cost centre

C   charge overheads to products

D   control overheads

32 Cartcycle Ltd's budgeted overheads in the wood cutting department were £586,792. The overheads are absorbed based on machine hours. The budgeted machine hours were 9,464 and the actual machine hours were 9,745. The actual overhead cost was £568,631

(a) **What is the overhead absorption rate?**

A   £62 per machine hour

B   £60 per machine hour

C   £58 per machine hour

D   £55 per machine hour

(b) **How much overhead was absorbed?**

A   £584,700

B   £586,768

C   £604,190

D   £565,210

(c) **What is the under or over absorbed amount?**

A   £35,559 over

B   £35,599 under

C   £21,582 over

D   £21,582 under

33   Next quarter Aquarius Ltd's budgeted overheads and activity levels are:

	Assembly	Finishing
Budgeted overheads (£)	155,000	105,000
Budgeted direct labour hours	12,500	8,750
Budgeted machine hours	2,000	1,750

(a)   **What would the budgeted overhead absorption rate be for each department, if this were set based on their both being heavily automated?**

   A   Assembly £77.50/hour, Finishing £12/hour

   B   Assembly £77.50/hour, Finishing £60/hour

   C   Assembly £12.40/hour, Finishing £60/hour

   D   Assembly £12.40/hour, Finishing £12/hour

(b)   **What would the budgeted overhead absorption rate be for each department, if this were set based on their both being labour intensive?**

   A   Assembly £77.50/hour, Finishing £12/hour

   B   Assembly £77.50/hour, Finishing £60/hour

   C   Assembly £12.40/hour, Finishing £60/hour

   D   Assembly £12.40/hour, Finishing £12/hour

Additional data

At the end of the quarter actual overheads incurred in the finishing department were £119,000. Overheads were recovered on a machine hour basis. The machine hours worked were 10% less than budgeted.

(c)   **What was the under or over absorptions for finishing in the quarter?**

   £ _____   under/over absorbed

34   Next quarter Grape Limited's budgeted overheads and activity levels are:

	Moulding Dept	Painting Dept
Budgeted overheads (£)	36,000	39,000
Budgeted direct labour hours	9,000	13,000
Budgeted machine hours	18,000	1,200

(a)   **What would the budgeted overhead absorption rate be for each department, if the most appropriate basis was chosen?**

   A   Moulding £2/hour, Painting £32.50/hour

   B   Moulding £32.50/hour, Painting £2/hour

   C   Moulding £3/hour, Painting £33/hour

   D   Moulding £2/hour, Painting £3/hour

Additional data

At the end of the quarter actual overheads incurred were found to be:

	Moulding Dept	Painting Dept
Actual overheads (£)	37,500	40,000
Actual direct labour hours	9,500	13,500
Actual machine hours	17,500	700

(b) **How much overhead has been absorbed by each department?**

    A   Moulding £35,000, Painting £40,500

    B   Moulding £37,500 Painting £40,000

    C   Moulding £19,000, Painting £2,100

    D   Moulding £36,000, Painting £39,000

(c) **Using your answer from b what are the under or over absorptions in the quarter?**

    A   Moulding over absorbed £2,500, Painting over absorbed £500

    B   Moulding under absorbed £2,500, Painting over absorbed £500

    C   Moulding over absorbed £2,500, Painting under absorbed £500

    D   Moulding under absorbed £2,500, Painting under absorbed £500

35 **Next quarter Globe Limited's budgeted overheads and activity levels are:**

	Mixing Dept	Bagging Dept
Budgeted overheads (£)	64,800	70,200
Budgeted direct labour hours	1,620	2,340
Actual direct labour hours	1,840	2,120
Budgeted machine hours	10,000	12,000
Actual machine hours	9,000	13,000

(a) **What would the budgeted overhead absorption rate for each department, if the mixing department was heavily automated and the bagging department was labour intensive?**

    A   Mixing £6.48/hour, Bagging £30.00/hour

    B   Mixing £7.20/hour, Bagging £33.11/hour

    C   Mixing £6.48/hour, Bagging £5.85/hour

    D   Mixing £5.00/hour, Bagging £5.00/hour

(b) **How much overhead has been absorbed by production in each department?**

    A   Mixing £13,248, Bagging £70,193

    B   Mixing £58,320, Bagging £76,050

    C   Mixing £58,320, Bagging £63,600

    D   Mixing £64,800, Bagging £70,200

Additional data

At the end of the quarter actual overheads incurred were found to be:

	Mixing Dept	*Bagging Dept*
Actual overheads (£)	67,500	75,600

(c)   Using your answer from b what are the under or over absorptions in the quarter?

A   Mixing under absorbed £9,180, Bagging over absorbed £12,000

B   Mixing under absorbed £9,180, Bagging under absorbed £12,000

C   Mixing over absorbed £9,180, Bagging over absorbed £12,000

D   Mixing over absorbed £9,180, Bagging under absorbed £12,000

(d)   Complete the following sentence (*delete as appropriate)

An under absorption of overheads will be **debited/credited*** to the Profit and Loss account. This will **increase/decrease*** expenses and will **increase/decrease*** profit

36   Over-absorbed overheads occur when:

A   absorbed overheads exceed actual overheads

B   absorbed overheads exceed budgeted overheads

C   actual overheads exceed budgeted overheads

D   budgeted overheads exceed absorbed overheads

37   The management accountant's report shows that fixed production overheads were over-absorbed in the last accounting period. The combination that is certain to lead to this situation is:

A   production volume is lower than budget and actual expenditure is higher than budget

B   production volume is higher than budget and actual expenditure is higher than budget

C   production volume and actual cost are as budgeted

D   production volume is higher than budget and actual expenditure is lower than budget

ACTIVITY BASED COSTING

38   **The following statements have been made about ABC and cost drivers.**

(1)   A cost driver is any factor that causes a change in the cost of an activity.

(2)   For long-term variable overhead costs, the cost driver could be the volume of activity.

(3)   Traditional absorption costing tends to under-allocate overhead costs to low-volume products.

Which of the above statements is/are true?

A   (1) and (3) only

B   (2) and (3) only

C   (1) and (2) only

D   (1), (2) and (3)

39   The following statements have been made in relation to activity-based costing:

(1)   A cost driver is a factor which causes a change in the cost of an activity.

(2)   Traditional absorption costing tends to under-estimate overhead costs for high-volume products.

Which of the above statements is/are true?

A   (1) only

B   (2) only

C   Neither (1) nor (2)

D   Both (1) and (2)

40   The ABC Company manufactures two products, Product Alpha and Product Beta. Both are produced in a very labour-intensive environment and use similar processes. Alpha and Beta differ by volume. Beta is a high-volume product, while Alpha is a low-volume product. Details of product inputs, outputs and the costs of activities are as follows:

	Direct labour hours/unit	Annual output (units)	Number of purchase orders	Number of set-ups
Alpha	5	1,200	70	40
Beta	5	10,800	80	60
			150	100

Fixed overhead costs amount to a total of £420,000 and have been analysed as follows:

	£
Labour-related	90,000
Purchasing related	150,000
Set-up related	180,000

(a) Using a traditional method of overhead absorption based on labour hours, what is the overhead cost per unit for each unit of product Alpha?

    A   £7.00

    B   £24.91

    C   £35.00

    D   £125.83

(b) Using a traditional method of overhead absorption based on labour hours, what is the overhead cost per unit for each unit of product Beta?

    A   £7.00

    B   £24.91

    C   £35.00

    D   £125.83

(c) Using Activity Based Costing as method of overhead absorption, what is the overhead cost per unit for each unit of product Alpha?

    A   £7.00

    B   £24.91

    C   £35.00

    D   £125.83

(d) Using Activity Based Costing as method of overhead absorption, what is the overhead cost per unit for each unit of product Beta?

    A   £7.00

    B   £24.91

    C   £35.00

    D   £125.83

41   A company uses activity-based costing to calculate the unit cost of its products. The figures for Period 3 are as follows: production set-up costs are £84,000. Total production is 40,000 units of each of products A and B, and each run is 2,000 units of A or 5,000 units of B.

What is the set-up cost per unit of B?

    A   £0.10

    B   £0.08

    C   £0.60

    D   £0.29

42 DOG

Details of four products and relevant information are given below for one period:

Product	W	X	Y	Z
Output in units	240	200	160	240
Costs per unit	£	£	£	£
Direct material	80	100	60	120
Direct labour	56	42	28	42
Machine hours (per unit)	8	6	4	6

The production overhead is currently absorbed by using a machine hour rate, and the total of the production overhead for the period has been analysed as follows:

	£
Machine department costs	20,800
Set up costs	10,500
Stores receiving	7,200
Total	38,500

You have ascertained that the 'cost drivers' to be used are as listed below for the overhead costs shown:

Cost	Cost driver
Machine department costs	Machine hours
Set up costs	Number of production runs
Stores receiving	Requisitions raised

The four products are similar and are usually produced in production runs of 40 units.

The number of requisitions raised on the stores was 40 for each product.

Calculate the total cost and the cost per unit for each product, using activity based costing:

Total costs	W	X	Y	Z
	£	£	£	£
Direct materials				
Direct labour				
Machine department costs				
Set up costs				
Stores receiving				
Total cost				
Cost per unit				

ACTIVITY EFFECTS

COST BEHAVIOURS

43   **The following data relate to two output levels of a department:**

Machine hours	17,000	18,500
Overheads	£246,500	£251,750

The amount of fixed overheads is:

A   £5,250

B   £59,500

C   £187,000

D   £246,500

44   A manufacturing company has four types of cost (identified as T1, T2, T3 and T4).

The total cost for each type at two different production levels is:

Cost type	Total cost for 125 units	Total cost for 180 units
T1	£	£
T1	1,000	1,260
T2	1,750	2,520
T3	2,475	2,826
T4	3,225	4,644

Which two cost types would be classified as being semi-variable?

A   T1 and T3

B   T1 and T4

C   T2 and T3

D   T2 and T4

45 The following eight options describe the behaviour of different types of costs during a short period of one quarter of a year.

Option	Description	Option	Description
1	Decreases per unit as volume increases	5	Fixed for a certain volume range only
2	Increases per unit as selling price increases	6	Made up of fixed and variable costs
3	Variable for a certain volume range only	7	Increase in total as volume increases
4	Decreases in total as volume increases	8	Decreases per unit as selling price increases

What is the correct description for the following four types of cost?

	Description
Variable cost	
Fixed cost	
Stepped cost	
Semi-variable cost	

46 **Identify the TWO types of cost behaviour shown below:**

Graph 1

Total cost £

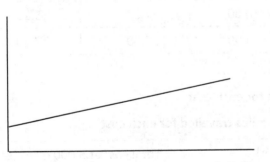

Activity

Graph 2

Total cost £

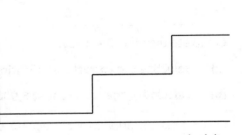

Activity

A   Variable

B   Fixed

C   Semi variable

D   Stepped fixed

A   Variable

B   Fixed

C   Semi variable

D   Stepped fixed

47   **Why might a company decide to allocate its costs between the products of different departments?**

     A   To speed up internal reporting

     B   To comply with accounting standards

     C   To report segmented profits/losses

     D   To reduce its overall inventory valuation

48   **Complete the sentences below to show where specific reports will be sent.**

A **cost/profit** centre manager will be sent overall performance reports to monitor revenues.

Profit/investment centre managers will be sent reports detailing the returns on capital employed

A **cost/investment** centre manager will be sent details about amounts spent on maintaining machinery.

49   **TRUCK TRANSPORT**

Truck Transport Ltd is reviewing costs for the next month for contract Route NW. The cost analysis table below shows cost behaviour per miles travelled for four different cost classifications.

	Cost per mile travelled			
	1,500 miles	3,000 miles	4,500 miles	6,000 miles
Cost 1	14.00	7.00	6.00	4.50
Cost 2	7.00	7.00	7.00	7.00
Cost 3	21.00	10.50	7.00	5.25
Cost 4	12.00	9.00	8.00	7.50

Complete the table below by:

(a)   **selecting the correct classification for each cost**

(b)   **calculating the total cost at 5,000 miles travelled for each cost**

Cost	Classification (tick correct answer)				Total cost at 5,000 miles (£)
	Variable	Semi-variable	Fixed	Stepped fixed	
Cost 1					
Cost 2					
Cost 3					
Cost 4					

50 CARTCYCLE LTD

Cartcyle Ltd has prepared a forecast for the next quarter for one of its wooden products, DR43. This component is produced in batches and the forecast is based on selling and producing 2,160 batches.

One of the customers of Cartcyle Ltd has indicated that it may be significantly increasing its order level for product DR43 for the next quarter and it appears that activity levels of 2,700 batches and 3,600 batches are feasible.

The semi-variable costs should be calculated using the high-low method. If 5,400 batches are sold the total semi-variable cost will be £13,284, and there is a constant unit variable cost up to this volume.

Complete the table below and calculate the estimated profit per batch of DR43 at the different activity levels.

Batches produced and sold	2,160	2,700	3,600
	£	£	£
Sales revenue	64,800		
Variable costs:			
• Direct materials	9,720		
• Direct labour	22,680		
• Overheads	12,960		
Semi-variable costs:	6,804		
• Variable element			
• Fixed element			
Total cost	52,164		
Total profit	12,636		
Profit per batch (to 2 decimal places)	5.85		

51   CHARTER FLIGHTS

Charter Flights profit centre has just revised its forecasts for the number of miles it expects to fly during the next month on a particular charter contract. Originally it expected the contract would be for flights totalling 5,000 miles. Charter Flights now expects that the total miles to be flown will increase to either 6,000 or 7,000 miles.

Notes:

- The company chartering the flights has negotiated with Charter Flights a reduction of 10% per mile, paid on all miles flown in excess of the 5,000 miles agreed in the original contract.

- Landing and servicing fees are a semi-variable cost. There is a fixed charge of £600,000 plus £50/mile.

Complete the table below and calculate the estimated profit per mile flown at the different activity levels.

Likely miles	5,000	6,000	7,000
	£000	£000	£000
Sale revenue	2,500		
Variable/semi-variable costs:			
• Aviation fuel	400		
• Landing and servicing fees	850		
• Other variable overheads	135		
Fixed costs:			
• Wages and salaries	420		
• Other fixed overheads	625		
Total cost	2430		
Total profit	70		
Profit per mile flown (2 decimal places) £	14.00		

52 Grape Ltd is negotiating a new contract with a customer for one of its products – The Owl. Owl is produced in batches and the forecast is based on selling and producing 800 batches.

The customer has indicated that it may be increasing its order level for Owl for the next quarter and it appears that activity levels of 1,200 units and 1,500 units are feasible.

The semi-variable costs should be calculated using the high-low method. If 1,600 batches are sold the total semi-variable cost will be £4,920, and there is a constant unit variable cost up to this volume.

Revenues and costs for 800 Owls are shown below. Fixed costs remain constant through the range being considered.

Units produced and sold	800
	£
Sales revenue	24,000
Variable costs:	
• Direct materials	3,600
• Direct labour	8,400
• Overheads	1,800
Semi-variable costs	2,520
Total cost	16,320
Total profit	7,680
Profit per batch (to 2 decimal places)	9.60

Calculate the following:

(a) The sales revenue per unit if the contract is for 800 Owls

(b) The variable cost per unit if the contract is for 1,200 Owls

(c) The fixed cost per unit if the contract is for 1,200 Owls

(d) The total cost per unit if the contract is for 1,500 Owls

(e) The profit per unit if the contract is for 1,500 Owls

SEGMENTAL REPORTS

53 Truck Transport Ltd is planning new routes for the next month, Route S, Route SE and Route SW. The following data has been put together for the routes.

1   The contract for Route S is for 3,000 miles and the rate is £150 per mile

The contract for Route SE is for 20% less miles that Route S with a rate of 10% more.

The contract for Route SW is for 20% more miles that Route S with a rate of 10% less.

2   Variable costs are £80 per mile for Route S

Variable costs are £5 more per mile for Route SE than Route S

Variable costs are 6.25% less per mile for Route SW than Route S

3   The fixed costs for the contracts will total £400,000 to be apportioned 20% to Route S, 30% to Route SE and the remainder to Route SW.

(a)   You are required to complete the following table to show the forecast contribution and profit for the three new routes.

	Route S	Route SE	Route SW
Contract miles			
Revenue and costs			
Revenue (£000s)			
Variable costs (£000s)			
Contribution (£000)			
Fixed costs (£000)			
Profit (£000s)			

(b)   Looking at the information in part (a), indicate how you should react to the following scenario by ticking yes or no in the table.

Scenario	Yes	No
You are asked to change the variable cost figure to increase profit. There is no evidence to support the change in cost. Do you do this?		
You discover an error that will significantly impact the profit for one of the routes. Do you report this to your manager?		
While completing the forecast you wonder why the different routes are charged different rates per mile. Do you ask your manager to explain?		
A friend of the family works for a competitor and would like to see your forecast calculations. Do you let them see?		

54 INDIA LTD

India Ltd manufactures and sells three ranges of pottery, Rose, Tulip and Buttercup. The following information has been provided for the next quarter.

	Rose	Tulip	Buttercup
Sales revenue (£)	50,000	24,000	40,000
Direct materials (£)	10,000	4,800	8,000
Direct labour (£)	13,000	8,800	10,500

India Ltd expects to produce and sell 1,000 units of Rose and 200 units of Tulip. The budgeted sales demand for Buttercup is 50% less than that of Rose. Budgeted total fixed costs are £52,000.

Complete the table below (to two decimal places) to show the budgeted contribution per unit for the three products and the company's budgeted profit or loss for the year.

	Rose (£)	Tulip (£)	Buttercup (£)	Total (£)
Selling price per unit				
Less: Variable costs per units				
Direct material				
Direct labour				
Contribution per unit				
Sales volume (units)				
Total contribution				
Less: fixed costs				
Budgeted profit/loss				

55 SPORT SHIRT LTD

Sport Shirts Ltd has provided the following cost and sales information for a new range and an existing range of sports shirts:

	New	Existing
Sales and production units	2,000	3,000
Labour hours per month	500	1,500
Unit selling price	£12.00	£20.00
Unit material cost	£3.75	£4.00
Unit direct labour cost	£1.25	£2.50

The company expects its monthly fixed costs to be as follows:

- Production   £11,400
- Sales   £12,100
- Administration   £10,250

(a) Complete the table below to calculate the forecast total monthly contribution and total profit for the company from the sale and production of both shirt ranges.

	New £	Existing £	Total £
Sales revenue			
Less: variable costs			
Direct materials			
Direct labour			
Total contribution			
Less: fixed costs			
Budgeted profit/loss			

(b) Which of these is an example of unethical behaviour by one of Sport shirt's accounting technicians?

A   Treating Sport shirt's costs as confidential

B   Calculating profits subjectively rather than objectively

C   Valuing inventory in a consistent manner period to period

D   Allocating costs between products objectively

SHORT TERM DECISION MAKING

COST VOLUME PROFIT ANALYSIS

56   Choose the correct description for each of the following:

Term
Contribution
Breakeven point
Margin of safety

Description
Excess of actual sales over breakeven sales
Selling price less variable costs
Sales units where is no profit or loss

57   Cartcycle Ltd has the following budgeted costs per unit for product MR13:

		£
Variable costs	Direct material	7.50
	Direct labour	8.00
	Overheads	11.50
Total variable costs		27.00
Fixed costs	Overheads	7.20
Total costs		34.20

Product MR13 has a selling price of £41.40 per unit. Budgeted sales volume is 9,000 units.

(a)   Calculate the budgeted fixed overheads for product MR13.

> £ ☐

(b)   Calculate the budgeted breakeven volume, in units, for product MR13.

> ☐ units

(c)   Complete the table below to show the budgeted margin of safety in units and the margin of safety percentage if Cartcyle Ltd sells 9,000 units of product MR13.

Units of MR13 sold	9,000
Margin of safety (units)	
Margin of safety percentage (2dp)	

(d)   If Cartcyle Ltd increases the selling price of MR13 by £1.80 what will be the impact on the breakeven point and the margin of safety assuming no change in the number of units sold?

A   The breakeven point will decrease and the margin of safety will increase

B   The breakeven point will stay the same but the margin of safety will decrease

C   The breakeven point will decrease and the margin of safety will stay the same

D   The breakeven point will increase and the margin of safety will decrease

Cartcycle Ltd wishes to make a profit of £36,000 on the sale of MR13

(e)   Complete the table below to calculate the number of units that Cartcycle Ltd must sell to achieve its target profit, the margin of safety (%) and the margin of safety in sales revenue for the target profit assuming that the sales demand, selling price and all costs remain as per budget.

	Product MR13
Number of units to be sold to meet target profit	
Revised margin of safety to 2 decimal places (%)	
Revised margin of safety in sales revenue (£)	

58   Seafood soup sells for 80p per can. It has a marginal cost of production of 30p per can. Fixed costs attributable to this range of soups total £312,500.

(a)   Calculate the sales revenue of seafood soup CCS has to achieve to break even.

£ [   ]

(b)   Calculate the sales revenue of seafood soup CCS needs to achieve to make a profit of £200,000.

£ [   ]

(c)   If CCS were to sell £875,000 worth of seafood soup, what would be:

(i)   the margin of safety

£ [   ]

(ii)   the margin of safety percentage over the break-even sales?

[   ] %

59   The following budgeted annual sales and cost information relates to labelled food containers types A and B:

Product	A	B
Units made and sold	300,000	500,000
Machine hours required	60,000	40,000
Sales revenue (£)	450,000	600,000
Direct materials (£)	60,000	125,000
Direct labour (£)	36,000	70,000
Variable overheads (£)	45,000	95,000

Total fixed costs attributable to A and B are budgeted to be £264,020.

(a)   Complete the table below (to 2 decimal places) to show the budgeted contribution per unit of A and B sold, and the company's budgeted profit or loss for the year from these two products.

	A (£)	B (£)	Total (£)
Selling price per unit			
Less: variable costs per unit			
Direct materials			
Direct labour			
Variable overheads			
Contribution per unit			
Sales volume (units)			
Total contribution			
Less: fixed costs			
Budgeted profit or loss			

The £264,020 of fixed costs attributed to products A and B can be split between the two products: £158,620 to A and £105,400 to B.

The latest sales forecast is that 250,000 units of product A and 400,000 units of product B will be sold during the year.

(b) **Using your calculations and the additional data above, complete the table below to calculate:**

Product	A	B
Fixed costs (£)		
Unit contribution (£)		
Break-even sales (units)		
Forecast sales (units)		
Margin of safety (units)		
Margin of safety (%)		

(c) **Which of the 2 products has the safer margin of safety?**

Product A		Product B	

60 Eastern Bus Company (ECB) has produced three forecasts of miles to be driven during the next three months for a particular contract. The original contract is for journeys totalling 10,000 miles. It now seems likely, however, that the total journeys involved will increase to either 12,000 or 14,000 miles.

(a) **Complete the table below in order to estimate the profit per mile (in pounds, to 3 decimal places) of this contract for the three likely mileages.**

Likely miles	10,000	12,000	14,000
	£	£	£
Sales revenue	100,000		
Variable costs:			
• Fuel	8,000		
• Drivers' wages and associated costs	5,000		
• Overheads	6,000		
Fixed costs:			
• Indirect labour	10,600		
• Overheads	25,850		
Total cost	55,450		
Total profit	44,550		
Profit per mile	4.455		

(b)   **Using the information provided above and your own calculations for that task, calculate:**

Forecast number of miles		12,000	14,000
Sales revenue	£		
Fixed costs	£		
Contribution	£		
Contribution per mile	£		
Break-even number of miles	Miles		
Break-even sales revenue	£		
Margin of safety in number of miles	Miles		
Margin of safety in sales revenue	£		
Margin of safety	%		

61   Four lines representing expected costs and revenues have been drawn on a breakeven chart:

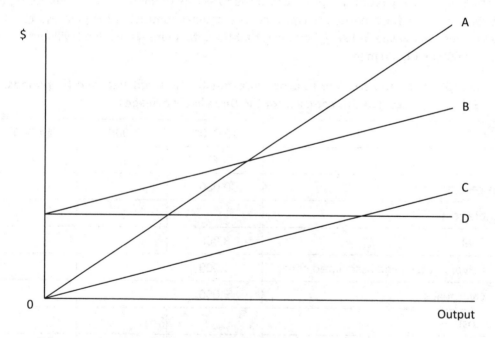

Match the line letter with the correct description?

A		Fixed costs
B		Total revenue
C		Total costs
D		Total variable costs

62 Jump Ltd manufactures wooden poles. One length (0.8m) of pole is produced in batches of 150 poles. Each pole is sold for £10. The following are the costs involved in its manufacture:

Batch of 150 0.8m poles	£
Direct material	75
Direct labour	200
Variable overheads	250
Fixed overheads	325

(a)   **Calculate the breakeven volume of 0.8m poles:**

(b)   **Calculate the breakeven sales revenue of 0.8m poles**

Jump Ltd also manufactures 2.8m poles. This is manufactured in batches of 50 poles and makes a contribution of £1,500 per batch. Fixed costs are £450. Jump Ltd has set a target profit of £2,400 from manufacture and selling this pole.

(c)   **How many 2.8m poles must Jump sell to reach its target profit of £2,400**

(d)   **Calculate the margin of safety of the 2.8m pole (in poles)**

LIMITING FACTOR ANALYSIS

63 A company manufactures two products (L and M) using the same material and labour. It holds no inventory. Information about the variable costs and maximum demands are as follows:

	Product L	Product M
Material (litre)	3.25	4.75
Labour (hour)	5	4
Maximum monthly demand (units)	6,000	8,000

Each month 50,000 litres of material and 60,000 labour hours are available.

Which one of the following statements is correct?

A   Material is a limiting factor but labour is not a limiting factor

B   Material is not a limiting factor but labour is a limiting factor

C   Neither material nor labour is a limiting factor

D   Both material and labour are limiting factors

64 Yeknom makes two products, the apple breakfast bar and the banana breakfast bar. The following budgeted annual sales and cost information relates to a and b:

Product	Apple bars	Banana bars
Bars made and sold	75,000	125,000
Machine hours required	30,000	20,000
Sales revenue(£)	225,000	300,000
Direct materials (£)	30,000	62,500
Direct labour (£)	18,000	35,000
Variable overheads (£)	22,500	47,500
Fixed overheads (£)	150,000	

(a) **Complete the table below (to 2 decimal places) to show the budgeted contribution per bar of Apple and bar of Banana sold, and the company's budgeted profit or loss for the year from these two products.**

	Apple (£)	Banana (£)	Total (£)
Selling price per bar			
Less: variable costs per unit			
Direct materials			
Direct labour			
Variable overheads			
Contribution per unit			
Sales volume (bars)			
Total contribution			
Less: fixed costs			
Budgeted profit or loss			

Due to a machine breakdown the number of machine hours available for products Apple bars and Banana bars has now been reduced to only 35,000 during the year.

(b) **Given this limitation and your calculations, complete the table below to recommend how many bars of products Apple and Banana Yeknom should now make in order to maximise the profit from these two products for the year.**

Product	Apple bars	Banana bars	Total
Contribution/unit (£)			
Machine hours/unit			
Contribution/machine hour (£)			
Product ranking			
Machine hours available			
Machine hours allocated to: Product .... Product			
Units made			
Total contribution			
Less: fixed costs (£)			
Profit/loss made (£)			

65 Monty makes two products, the Squeaker and the Hooter. The following budgeted annual sales and cost information relates to the Squeaker and the Hooter:

Product	Squeaker	Hooter
Contribution	20,000	24,500
Fixed costs (£)	7,000	8,000
Profit from operations(£)	13,000	16,500
Units produced	80,000	70,000
Machine hours required	40,000	17,500

Due to a machine breakdown the number of machine hours available for production has now been reduced to only 50,000 during the year.

(a) **Given this limitation complete the table below to recommend how many units of Squeakers and Hooters Monty should now make in order to maximise the profit from these two products for the year.**

Product	Squeakers	Hooters	Total
Contribution per unit (£)			
Contribution per machine hour (£)			
Ranking			
Total machine hours available			
Machine hours allocated to			
Units made			
Total contribution earned (£)			
Less: fixed costs (£)			
Forecast profit/loss made (£)			

(b) **Complete the following sentence, using your results from (a) above.**

Hooters should be selected as the first product to be made as it has the **highest**/lowest* contribution per unit/**contribution per machine hour***

66 Three of CPL's products use the same rare plant extract as part of their manufacture. The sole supplier has informed CPL that, due to flooding at its South American facility, they can only supply 6,000 kgs of the plant extract next month.

The following is the budget information about the three affected products for next month:

Product	AB1	CD2	EF3	Total
	£	£	£	£
Contribution	26,400	34,600	48,204	109,204
Fixed costs allocated or apportioned	7,430	9,750	13,600	30,780
Profit	18,970	24,850	34,604	78,424
Number of packs to be sold	6,600	6,920	16,068	
Kgs of plant extract required	2,640	1,730	8,034	

Complete the table below to advise how many packs of each product should actually be produced next month to maximise profits during this period.

Product	AB1	CD2	EF3	Total
Contribution/pack (£)				
Kgs of plant extract/pack				
Contribution/kg (£)				
Product ranking				
Kgs of plant extract available				
Kgs allocated to each product				
Number of packs to produce				
Total contribution earned (£)				
Less: Fixed costs (£)				
Profit/loss made (£)				

67 Asparagus soup and broccoli soup have the following budgeted annual sales and cost information:

Product	Asparagus soup	Broccoli soup
Cans made and sold	1,200,000	1,800,000
Machine hours required	6,000	9,000
Sales revenue (£)	720,000	900,000
Direct materials (£)	84,000	108,000
Direct labour (£)	72,000	126,000
Variable overheads (£)	24,000	54,000
Fixed overheads attributable to both types of soup (£)	652,000	

(a)   Complete the table below (in pence) to show the budgeted contribution per can for both types of soup, and the company's budgeted profit or loss for the year from these two products (in £).

	Asparagus soup	Broccoli soup	
	p	p	
Selling price per can			
Less: variable costs per can			
Direct materials			
Direct labour			
Variable overheads			
Contribution per can			
	No of cans	No of cans	
Sales volume (cans)			
	£	£	Total (£)
Total contribution			
Less: fixed costs			
Budgeted profit or loss			

Due to a machine breakdown the number of machine hours available for production has now been reduced to only 12,000 during the year.

(b)   Given this limitation and your calculations, complete the table below to recommend how many cans of Asparagus soup and Broccoli soup CPL should now make in order to maximise the profit from these two products for the year.

Product	Asparagus soup	Broccoli soup	Total
Contribution/can (£)			
Machine hours/can			
Contribution/machine hour (£)			
Product ranking			
Machine hours available			
Machine hours allocated to:			
Product			
Product			
Units made			
Total contribution			
Less: fixed costs (£)			
Profit/loss made (£)			

TYPES OF COSTING SYSTEMS

JOB, BATCH AND SERVICE COSTING

68   A company operates a job costing system. Job 812 requires £60 of direct materials, £40 of direct labour and £20 of direct expenses. Direct labour is paid £8 per hour. Production overheads are absorbed at a rate of £16 per direct labour hour and non-production overheads are absorbed at a rate of 60% of prime cost.

   What is the total cost of Job 812?

   A   £240

   B   £260

   C   £272

   D   £320

69   A business operates a batch costing system. The prime cost of a batch was £6,840 and it had used 156 direct labour hours. The fixed production overheads are absorbed on the basis of direct labour hours. The budgeted overhead absorption rate was based upon a budgeted fixed overhead of £300,000 and total budgeted direct labour hours of 60,000. The batch contained 500 items.

   What is the cost per unit in the batch?

£

70   A hotel calculates a number of statistics including average cost per occupied bed per day.

   The following information is provided for a 30-day period.

	Rooms with twin beds	Single rooms
Number of rooms in hotel	260	70
Number of rooms available to let	240	40
Average number of rooms occupied daily	200	30

Number of guests in period	6,450
Average length of stay	2 days
Payroll costs for period	£100,000
Cost of cleaning supplies in period	£5,000
Total cost of laundering in period	£22,500

   The average cost per occupied bed per day for the period is:

   A   £9.90

   B   £9.88

   C   £7.20

   D   £8.17

71 **Which of the following are features of service organisations?**

(i)   High levels of inventory

(ii)   High proportion of fixed costs

(iii)   Difficulty in identifying suitable cost units

A   (i) and (ii) only

B   (i) and (iii) only

C   (ii) and (iii) only

D   All of these

PROCESS COSTING – LOSSES/GAINS

72 **CARTCYCLE LTD**

The Wood finishing department of Cartcyle Ltd uses process costing for some of its products.

The process account for July for one particular process has been partly completed but the following information is also relevant:

Two employees worked on this process during July. Each employee worked 40 hours per week for 4 weeks and was paid £18 per hour.

Overheads are absorbed on the basis of £28.80 per labour hour.

Cartcyle Ltd expects a normal loss of 5% during this process, which it then sells for scrap at £1.08 per kg.

(a)   **Complete the process account below for July. Show total costs to the nearest £ and unit costs to 3 decimal places**

Description	Kgs	Unit cost £	Total cost £	Description	Kgs	Unit cost £	Total cost £
Material TR	1,080	2.16		Normal loss		1.08	
Material DG	720	2.70		Output	2,300		
Material IG	720	1.10					
Labour							
Overheads							

(b)   **Identify the correct entry for each of the following in a process account.**

	Debit	Credit
Abnormal loss		
Abnormal gain		

73 **In process costing, if an abnormal loss arises the process account is generally:**

A   debited with the scrap value of the abnormal loss units

B   debited with the full production cost of the abnormal loss units

C   credited with the scrap value of the abnormal loss units

D   credited with the full production cost of the abnormal loss units

74 The metal finishing department of Aquarius Ltd uses process costing for its product.

The material requirements are:

Material CBB – 700 kilograms @ £1.30 per kilogram

Material BSS – 500 kilograms @ £1.12 per kilogram

Material SMA – 500 kilograms @ £0.72 per kilogram

(a)   **Complete the table below to show the total cost of the materials input into the process.**

	£
Material CBB	
Material BSS	
Material SMA	

Aquarius Ltd estimate that the process two employees to work on this process. Each employee will work 40 hours per week for 4 weeks and be paid £8 per hour.

Overheads are absorbed on the basis of £12 per labour hour.

(b)   **Calculate the total labour cost and total overhead cost**

Total labour cost £	Total overhead cost £

(c)   **Calculate the total quantity and value of inputs into the process**

Total quantity (kg)	Total cost £

Aquarius Ltd expects a normal loss of 2% during this process, which it then sells for scrap at 50p per kg.

(d)   **Calculate the total scrap value of the normal loss**

Value of scrap £

(e)   **Calculate the cost per kilogram of output assuming a normal loss of 2% of input. State your answer to 2 decimal places.**

Cost per kilogram £

(f)   **If output is 1,600 calculate if there has been an abnormal loss or gain, the quantity of the loss or gain and the value of the loss**

Abnormal loss or gain	Quantity of loss or gain (kg)	Value of loss or gain (£)

75   GRAPE LTD

The Glazing department of Grape Ltd uses process costing for glazing finished statues.

The process account for January for one particular process has been partly completed but the following information is also relevant:

Four employees worked on this process during January. Each employee worked 30 hours per week for 4 weeks and was paid £12 per hour.

Overheads are absorbed on the basis of £8 per labour hour.

Grape Ltd expects a normal loss of 10% during this process, which it then sells for scrap at £5 per kg.

Complete the process account below for January. Show total costs to the nearest £ and unit costs to 2 decimal places.

Description	Units	Unit cost £	Total cost £	Description	Units	Unit cost £	Total cost £
Input – Statues	300	11.25	3,375	Normal loss		5.00	
Materials – Glaze			500	Output	290		
Labour							
Overheads							

76   Last month one of CPL's products had the following process inputs:

- Direct materials   500 kgs at £17.20 per kg
- Direct labour   280 labour hours at £10.50 per hour
- Overheads absorbed   86 machine hours at £32 per machine hour

The following information is also available:

- The company expects a normal loss of 5% of input.
- All waste is sold for £1.68 per kg.
- Actual output for the month was 490 kgs.
- There were no opening or closing inventory and all output was fully completed.

(a)   **Calculate the product's cost per kg of normal production.**

£	per kg

(b) **Prepare the process account below for the product for last month:**

Description	Kgs	Unit cost £	Total cost £		Description	Kgs	Unit cost £	Total cost £
Materials					Output			
Labour					Normal loss			
Overheads								

PROCESS COSTING – EQUIVALENT UNITS

77 Bahadra makes biscuits. Production requires several successive processes and the production details of the first process are as follows:

Volume completed in period	5,000 kg
Closing work in process	600 kg
Degree of completion of closing WIP:	
Materials	100%
Labour	50%
Overheads	50%
Costs incurred in April:	
Materials	£56,000
Labour	£26,500
Overheads	£10,600

Calculate the cost per equivalent units for materials and conversion

	Materials	Conversion
Cost per EU		

78 Parry makes bungee cords. Production requires several successive processes and the production details of the first process are as follows:

Volume completed in period	9,000 units
Closing work in process	3,500 units
Degree of completion of closing WIP:	
Materials	100%
Labour	75%
Overheads	75%
Costs incurred in April:	
Materials	£18,750
Labour	£12,415
Overheads	£16,415

Calculate the cost of the completed output and closing WIP

	Completed output	Closing WIP
Cost £		

79   The following data relates to work in progress stocks of solvent S789 during November:

Opening work in progress	Nil
Finished output to next process	7,000 litres
Closing work in progress	1,200 litres
Degree of completion – direct materials	100%
Degree of completion – direct labour	50%

The total labour cost is £3,800.

The direct labour cost per litre of solvent S789 of the equivalent finished production is:

A   £0.46

B   £0.50

C   £0.60

D   £0.63

80   There were 300 units of closing work in progress at the end of period 2 which was 80% complete with regards materials and 60% complete with regards conversion.

How much work, in equivalent units, is required to complete the Opening WIP in period 3?

	Material	Conversion
EU to complete OWIP		

81   There are 200 units of opening work in progress at the start of period 6 which is 100% complete with regards materials and 45% complete with regards conversion.

How much work, in equivalent units, is required to complete the Opening WIP in period 6?

	Material	Conversion
EU to complete OWIP		

82 Squid makes fountain pens on a production line. The details of the process in Period 2 are as follows:

Opening WIP =   300 units

Costs incurred so far

        Materials   £1,150

        Conversion   £2,700

Degrees of completion

        Materials   100%

        Conversion   60%

700 units were input at the start of the period

Completed output =   800 units

Closing WIP =   200 units

Degrees of completion

        Materials   100%

        Conversion   70%

Costs incurred in Period 2:

        Materials   £2,170

        Conversion   £4,484

(a) **Calculate the cost per equivalent unit for materials and conversion using the FIFO method of valuing OWIP (to 2 decimal places).**

	Material	Conversion
Cost per EU £		

(b) **Calculate the value of the completed output and the CWIP using the FIFO method of valuing OWIP (nearest whole £).**

	Completed output	CWIP
Value £		

83 A factory manufactures fizzy drinks. During October work 7,000 litres were input into a process.

OWIP = 2,000 litres

Costs incurred so far

Materials	£4,000
Conversion	£1,950

Degrees of completion

Materials	100%
Conversion	50%

Completed output = 8,000 litres

Costs incurred in Period:

Materials	£9,500
Conversion	£7,080

Closing WIP = 1,000 litres

Degrees of completion

Materials	100%
Conversion	60%

(a) **Calculate the cost per equivalent unit for materials and conversion using the AVCO method of valuing OWIP (to 2 decimal places).**

	Material	Conversion
Cost per EU £		

(b) **Calculate the value of the completed output and the CWIP using the AVCO method of valuing OWIP (nearest whole £).**

	Completed output	CWIP
Value £		

ABSORPTION AND MARGINAL COSTING

84 **Which of the following are true of marginal costing?**

(i) The marginal cost of a product includes an allowance for fixed production costs.

(ii) The marginal cost of a product represents the additional cost of producing an extra unit.

(iii) If the inventory increases over a year, the profits under absorption costing will be lower than with marginal costing.

A (i) only

B (ii) only

C (ii) and (iii) only

D (i), (ii) and (iii)

85 **Which of these statements are true of marginal costing?**

(i) The contribution per unit will be constant if the sales volume increases.

(ii) There is no under–or over–absorption of overheads.

(iii) Marginal costing does not provide useful information for decision making.

A (i) and (ii) only

B (ii) and (iii) only

C (ii) only

D (i), (ii) and (iii)

86 The following information relates to a contract for transporting school children during May 20X7:

	£
Fuel and other variable overheads	9,200
Fixed costs:	
Drivers' wages, pension and national insurance	3,220
Other fixed overheads	23,000
Number of miles travelled	4,600

Calculate the cost per mile under:

(a) Marginal costing

> £

(b) Absorption costing

> £

87 Globe Ltd has prepared a forecast for the next quarter for Tomato fertilizer.

Globe budgets to produce 1,800kg of the fertiliser and sell 1,000kg. The cost and revenue for this budget is as follows:

	£000
Sales	50,000
Direct materials	7,560
Direct labour	17,640
Fixed production overheads	3,600
Advertising (fixed cost)	2,010

Globe has no opening inventory of the fertilizer.

Produce a marginal costing statement of profit or loss and an absorption costing statement of profit or loss:

Marginal costing	£000	£000
Sales		
Opening inventory		
Production costs		
Less: Closing inventory		
Less: Cost of sales		
Contribution		
Less: Fixed costs		
Profit for the period		

Absorption costing	£000	£000
Sales		
Opening inventory		
Production costs		
Less: Closing inventory		
Less: Cost of sales		
Gross profit		
Less: Non-production cost		
Profit for the period		

88 ILCB has the following information relating to one of its products:

• Selling price per unit	£12
• Prime cost per unit	£4
• Variable production overhead cost per unit	£3
• Budgeted fixed production overhead	£30,000 per month
• Budgeted production	15,000 units per month
• Budgeted sales	12,000 units per month
• Opening inventory	2,000 units

(a) **Produce a marginal costing statement of profit or loss**

Marginal costing	£	£
Sales		
Opening inventory		
Production costs		
Less: Closing inventory		
Less: Cost of sales		
Contribution		
Less: Fixed costs		
Profit for the period		

(b) **What would the profit be under absorption costing principles?**

£

89 CPL is considering what the effect would be of costing its products under marginal costing principles, instead of under absorption costing principles that it currently follows:

The following information relates to one of the company's products:

Selling price per unit	£40
Prime cost per unit	£12
Variable production overhead cost per unit	£4
Budgeted fixed production overhead	£120,000 per month
Budgeted production	12,000 units per month
Budgeted sales	10,000 per month
Opening inventory	500 units

(a) **Calculate the contribution per unit:**

£

(b) **Calculate the profit per unit:**

£

(c) **Complete the table below to produce a statement of profit or loss for the product for the month under absorption costing principles.**

Absorption costing	£	£
Sales		
Opening inventory		
Production costs		
Less: Closing inventory		
Less: Cost of sales		
Gross profit		
Less: Non-production cost		
Profit for the period		

(d) **What would the profit be under marginal costing principles?**

£

90 A new company has set up a marginal costing system and has a budgeted profit for the period of £23,000 based on sales of 13,000 units and production of 15,000 units. This level of production represents the firm's expected long-term level of production. The company's budgeted fixed production costs are £3,000 for the period.

If the company were to change to an absorption costing system the budgeted profit would be:

A £22,600

B £23,400

C £25,600

D £26,400

91 Jump Ltd is planning to launch a new painted pole. It will be manufactured in batches of 100.

The following cost estimates have been produced per batch of painted pole:

	£
Direct material	4,500
Direct labour	5,000
Variable production overheads	2,500
Fixed production overheads	1,750
Administration, selling and distribution costs	2,250

(a) **Calculate the estimated prime cost per batch of painted poles**

£ [   ]

(b) **Calculate the estimated marginal production cost per batch of painted poles**

£ [   ]

(c) **Calculate the estimated full absorption cost of one batch of painted poles**

£ [   ]

The pole painting department is a cost centre

(d) **Which of the following does its management control (tick all that apply)?**

	Tick
Variable costs	
Fixed costs	
Sales revenue	
Assets and liabilities	

BASIC VARIANCE ANALYSIS

VARIANCE ANALYSIS

92 **Which of the following statements are correct?**

(i)   An adverse variance increases profit

(ii)   A favourable variance increases profit

(iii) A favourable variance will arise when actual revenue is greater than budgeted revenue

(iv)   An adverse variance will arise when actual costs are greater than budgeted costs

Options:

A   (i) only

B   (ii) only

C   (i), (iii) and (iv)

D   (ii), (iii) and (iv)

93   AQUARIUS LTD

Aquarius Ltd. has the following original budget and actual performance for product Britz for the year ending 31 December.

	Budget	Actual
Volume sold	200,000	267,000
	£000	£000
Sales revenue	1,600	2,409
Less costs:		
Direct materials	400	801
Direct labour	200	267
Fixed overheads	600	750
Profit from operations	400	591

Complete the table below to show a flexed budget and the resulting variances against this budget for the year. Show the actual variance amount, for sales and each cost, in the column headed 'Variance' and indicate whether this is Favourable or Adverse by entering F or A in the final column. If neither F nor A enter 0.

	Flexed budget	Actual	Variance	Favourable (F) or Adverse (A)
Volume sold		267,000		
	£000	£000	£000	
Sales revenue		2,409		
Less costs:				
Direct materials		801		
Direct labour		267		
Fixed overheads		750		
Profit from operations		591		

94   GRAPE LTD

Grape Ltd. has the following original budget and actual performance for product Bird Box Sets for the year ending 31 December.

(a)   **Complete the table below to show a flexed budget and the resulting variances against the budget for the year. Show the actual variance amount, for sales and each cost, in the column headed 'Variance'.**

Note:

- **Adverse variances must be denoted with a minus sign or brackets**

- **Enter 0 where any figure is zero.**

	Original budget	Flexed budget	Actual	Variance
Volume sold	20,000		28,800	
	£000	£000	£000	£000
Sales revenue	3,000		3,877	
Less costs:				
Direct materials	175		212	
Direct labour	875		912	
Variable overheads	445		448	
Fixed overheads	300		325	
Profit from operations	1,205		1,980	

(b)   **Referring to your answer for part (a), which one of the following has had the greatest impact in increasing the profit from operations?**

A   Sales revenue

B   Direct materials

C   Direct labour

D   Variable overheads

(c)   **Which of the following might have caused the variance for direct labour?**

A   An increase in units produced

B   An increase in employees' pay

C   Improved efficiency of employees

D   An increase in overtime

95   GLOBE LTD

Globe Ltd. has the following original budget and actual performance for product Bean for the year ending 31 December.

(a)   Complete the table below to show a flexed budget and the resulting variances against the budget for the year. Show the actual variance amount, for sales and each cost, in the column headed 'Variance'.

Note:

• Adverse variances must be denoted with a minus sign or brackets

• Enter 0 where any figure is zero.

	Original budget	Flexed budget	Actual	Variance
Volume sold	4,000		5,000	
	£000	£000	£000	£000
Sales revenue	1,500		1,950	
Less costs:				
Direct materials	36		45	
Direct labour	176		182	
Variable overheads	92		90	
Profit from operations	1,196		1,633	

(b)   Referring to your answer for part (a), which one of the following has had the least impact in increasing the profit from operations?

A   Sales revenue

B   Direct materials

C   Direct labour

D   Variable overheads

(c)   Which of the following might have caused the variance for sales revenue?

A   An increase in units produced

B   Offering a bulk discount

C   Increased competition from other companies

D   An increase in selling price

LONG TERM DECISION MAKING

PAYBACK, NPV AND IRR

96 Jump Ltd is considering a possible capital investment project. It will base its decision upon using three appraisal methods, the results re shown below:

Appraisal method	Notes	Company policy	Project results
Payback period		3 years	3.7 years
Net present value	Discount at 12% cost of capital	Accept if positive	12,000 +ve
Internal Rate of Return	Discount at 12% cost of capital	Must exceed cost of capital	14%

Identify the correct recommendation for each decision below:

Appraisal method	Recommendation
Payback period	
Net present value	
Internal Rate of Return	
Overall	

Options:

- Accept as greater than cost of capital

- Reject as greater than cost of capital

- Reject as per most important investment criterion

- Accept as per most important investment criterion

- Accept as positive

- Reject as positive

- Accept as more than 3 years

- Reject as more than 3 years

97 TRUCK TRANSPORT

Truck Transport Ltd has four possible investment opportunities but is only able to invest in two.

- The first investment needs to be risk limited

- The second investment should provide the best return for the shareholders possible.

The investment opportunities produce the following forecasts.

Method	Option 1	Option 2	Option 3	Option 4
Payback (years)	3.0	4.0	3.3	3.9
Net present value (£000)	16	21	36	52

(a) **Complete the sentences below by selecting the most appropriate choices from the options to advise Truck Transport of the options that should be chosen.**

For the first investment Truck Transport should invest in option **1 / 2 / 3 / 4** as it has the **highest NPV / lowest NPV/ longest payback period / shortest payback period**

For the second investment Truck Transport should invest in option **1 / 2 / 3 / 4** as it has the **highest NPV / lowest NPV / longest payback period / shortest payback period**

(b) **Review the statements below and identify whether they are true or false by ticking the correct option**

Statement	True	False
Payback method uses profits from a project to determine the payback period		
If the IRR is less than the cost of capital for a project, then it should be undertaken		
The IRR method uses discounted cash flows		
Projects with a negative NPV should be rejected		

98   CARTCYCLE

One of the finishing machines in Cartcycle Ltd's Wood finishing department is nearing the end of its useful life and the company is considering purchasing a replacement machine.

Estimates have been made for the initial capital cost, sales income and operating costs of the replacement machine, which is expected to have a useful life of three years:

	Year 0 £000	Year 1 £000	Year 2 £000	Year 3 £000
Capital expenditure	1,620			
Other cash flows:				
Sales income		756	1,008	1,440
Operating costs		216	270	342

The company appraises capital investment projects using a 15% cost of capital.

(a)   Complete the table below and calculate the net present value of the proposed replacement machine (to the nearest £000).

	Year 0 £000	Year 1 £000	Year 2 £000	Year 3 £000
Capital expenditure				
Sales income				
Operating costs				
Net cash flows				
PV factors	1.0000	0.8696	0.7561	0.6575
Discounted cash flows				
Net present value				

The net present value is *of positive/negative**

*delete as appropriate

(b)   Calculate the payback of the proposed replacement machine to the nearest whole month.

The payback period is   _____Year(s) and   _____Months

99   One of the finishing machines in Aquarius Ltd's metal finishing department is nearing the end of its useful life and the company is considering purchasing a replacement machine.

Estimates have been made for the initial capital cost, sales income and operating costs of the replacement machine, which is expected to have a useful life of three years:

	Year 0 £000	Year 1 £000	Year 2 £000	Year 3 £000
Capital expenditure	1,200			
Other cash flows:				
Sales income		530	570	710
Operating costs		140	160	170

The company appraises capital investment projects using a 15% cost of capital.

(a)   **Complete the table below and calculate the net present value of the proposed replacement machine (to the nearest £000).**

	Year 0 £000	Year 1 £00	Year 2 £000	Year 3 £000
Capital expenditure				
Sales income				
Operating costs				
Net cash flows				
PV factors	1.0000	0.8696	0.7561	0.6575
Discounted cash flows				
Net present value				

The net present value is *positive/negative**

*delete as appropriate

(b)   **If the net cash inflow in year 4 was £540,000, calculate the payback of the proposed replacement machine to the nearest whole month.**

The payback period is   _____Year(s) and   _____Months

100 One of the moulding machines in Grape Ltd's Moulding department is nearing the end of its useful life and the company is considering purchasing a replacement machine.

Estimates have been made for the initial capital cost, sales income and operating costs of the replacement machine, which is expected to have a useful life of three years:

	Year 0 £000	Year 1 £000	Year 2 £000	Year 3 £000
Capital expenditure	500			
Other cash flows:				
Sales income		280	330	370
Operating costs		100	120	140

The company appraises capital investment projects using a 10% cost of capital.

(a) **Complete the table below and calculate the net present value of the proposed replacement machine (to the nearest £000).**

	Year 0 £000	Year 1 £000	Year 2 £000	Year 3 £000
Capital expenditure				
Sales income				
Operating costs				
Net cash flows				
PV factors	1.0000	0.909	0.826	0.751
Discounted cash flows				
Net present value				

The net present value is *positive/negative**

*delete as appropriate

(b) **Estimate the IRR of this project**

A   0%

B   5%

C   10%

D   15%

(c) **Calculate the payback of the proposed replacement machine to the nearest whole month.**

The payback period is _____Year(s) and _____Months

101 BARTRUM LTD

Bartrum Ltd needs to purchase a new mashing machine. There are 2 machines available for purchase. Calculate the net present cost of each machine and recommend which machine should be purchased.

Machine A

	Year 0 £000	Year 1 £000	Year 2 £000	Year 3 £000
Capital expenditure	1,085			
Operating costs		200	200	200

Machine B

	Year 0 £000	Year 1 £000	Year 2 £000	Year 3 £000
Capital expenditure	1,200			
Operating costs		150	160	170

The company appraises capital investment projects using a 15% cost of capital.

Complete the tables below and calculate the net present cost of each of the proposed replacement machines (to the nearest £000).

Machine A

	Year 0 £000	Year 1 £000	Year 2 £000	Year 3 £000
Capital expenditure				
Net cash flows				
PV factors	1.0000	0.8696	0.7561	0.6575
Discounted cash flows				
Net present cost				

Machine B

	Year 0 £000	Year 1 £000	Year 2 £000	Year 3 £000
Capital expenditure				
Net cash flows				
PV factors	1.0000	0.8696	0.7561	0.6575
Discounted cash flows				
Net present cost				

Bartrum should invest in *Machine A/Machine B**

*delete as appropriate

102 CPL is considering replacing its fleet of delivery vehicles, and has produced the following estimates of capital expenditure and operating costs for two types of van. Both types of van are expected to have a three-year economic life.

Van type P	Year 0 £000	Year 1 £000	Year 2 £000	Year 3 £000
Capital expenditure	600			
Disposal proceeds				150
Operating costs		275	290	315

Van type R	Year 0 £000	Year 1 £000	Year 2 £000	Year 3 £000
Capital expenditure	750			
Disposal proceeds				170
Operating costs		345	365	390

The company's cost of capital is 16%.

Calculate the net present cost for both types of van. (Round the discounted cash flows to the nearest £000).

The net present cost of van type P

	Year 0 £000	Year 1 £000	Year 2 £000	Year 3 £000
Capital expenditure				
Disposal				
Net cash flows				
PV factors	1.0000	0.8621	0.7432	0.6407
Discounted cash flows				
Net present cost				

The net present cost of van type R

	Year 0 £000	Year 1 £000	Year 2 £000	Year 3 £000
Capital expenditure/disposal				
Net cash flows				
PV factors	1.0000	0.8621	0.7432	0.6407
Discounted cash flows				
Net present cost				

CPL should invest in *Van type P/Van type R* (*delete as appropriate)

103 **(a)** Globe Ltd's Finance Director has calculated an IRR of 12% for an investment opportunity. The company's required cost of capital is 15%. Should Globe Ltd take this investment opportunity?

Yes/No

(b) Globe Ltd's Finance Director has calculated an IRR of 17% for another investment opportunity. The companies required cost of capital is 15%. Should Globe Ltd take this investment opportunity?

Yes/No

(c) Globe Ltd's Finance Director has calculated an IRR of 15% for an investment opportunity. The companies required cost of capital is 15%. What is the value of the NPV?

£

104 A company is considering investing in a new mixing machine that will cost £3,000,000 to purchase but will reduce operating costs of the company. The following information is relevant to this decision:

- The payback period would be 2.4 years. The company's policy is for projects to pay back within 3 years.

- The net present value is £400,000 negative.

- The internal rate of return is 14%. The company's cost of capital is 16%.

Complete the report below, deleting words/phases where appropriate (marked with *)

REPORT

To: The Chief Accountant

From: AAT student

Subject: Investment appraisal

Date: 3 December 20X2

The payback period of 2.4 years is *within/outside** the company's policy of 3 years, and on this criterion the investment *should go/should not go** ahead.

The NPV is *positive/negative** and on this criterion the investment *should go/should not go** ahead.

The IRR, at 14%, is *above/below** the company's 16% cost of capital and on this criterion the investment *should go/should not go** ahead.

Overall the investment *should/should not** proceed because the *Payback/NPV/IRR** is the dominant criterion.

---

105 A company has determined that the net present value of an investment project is £17,706 when using a 10% discount rate and £(4,317) when using a discount rate of 15%.

Calculate the internal rate of return of the project to the nearest 1%.

%

106 An education authority is considering the implementation of a CCTV (closed circuit television) security system in one of its schools. Details of the proposed project are as follows:

Life of project	5 years
Initial cost	£75,000
Annual savings:	
Labour costs	£20,000
Other costs	£5,000
NPV at 15%	£8,800

The discount rates for 20% are:

Year	1	2	3	4	5
PV factors	0.833	0.694	0.579	0.482	0.402

Calculate the internal rate of return for this project to the nearest 1%

A   16%

B   18%

C   20%

D   22%

Section 2

ANSWERS TO PRACTICE QUESTIONS

INVENTORY

INVENTORY

1   A

The EOQ formula is $\sqrt{\dfrac{2 \times \text{cost of ordering} \times \text{annual demand}}{\text{Cost of holding one unit for one year}}}$

2   A

The cost of placing an order includes administrative costs, postage and quality control costs.

3   Maximum inventory level:

Re-order level = max usage × max lead time = 800 × 3 = 2,400

Re-order quantity = 500

Maximum = 2,400 + 500 − (500 × 1) = **2,400 units**

Minimum inventory level:

Re-order level = max usage × max lead time = 800 × 3 = 2,400

Average usage = (500 + 800)/2 = 650

Average lead time = (1 + 3)/2 = 2 weeks

Minimum = 2,400 − (650 × 2) = **1,100 units**

4 PLASTIC

(a)

$$\text{The EOQ} \sqrt{\frac{2 \times 3.60 \times 112.500}{1.80}} = 671$$

(b) Inventory record card

Date	Receipts Quantity kgs	Cost per kg (£)	Total cost (£)	Issues Quantity kgs	Cost per kg (p)	Total cost (£)	Balance Quantity kgs	Total cost (£)
Balance as at 22 July							198	238
24 July	671	2.336	1,567				869	1,805
26 July				540	1.920	1,037	329	768
28 July	671	2.344	1,573				1,000	2,341
30 July				710	2.341	1,662	290	679

Workings:

Issue on 26th July is made up of 198 @ 1.202 and 342 @ 2.336

Issue on 30th July is made up of 329 @ 2.336 and 381 @ 2.344

(d) 540 × £2.336 = **£1,261**

5 SURESTICK GLUE

(a) The EOQ = $\sqrt{\frac{2 \times 2.50 \times 2,500 \times 12}{1.00}} = 388$

(b) Inventory record card

Date	Receipts Quantity litres	Cost per litre	Total cost (£)	Issues Quantity litres	Cost per litre	Total cost (£)	Balance Quantity litres	Total cost (£)
Balance as at 23 June							65	130
24 June	388	2.234	867				453	997
26 June				180	2.201	397	273	600
27 June	388	2.341	909				661	1,509
30 June				250	2.283	571	411	938

(d) 180 × £2.234 = **£403**

6   GRAPE LTD

(a)   C – AVCO

(b)   Inventory record card

Date	Receipts			Issues			Balance	
	Drums	Cost per Drum (£)	Total cost (£)	Drums	Cost per drum (p)	Total cost (£)	Drums	Total cost (£)
Balance as at 22 January							1,650	1,980
25 January	1,200	1.250	1,500				2,850	3,480
26 January				1,300	1.221	1,587	1,550	1,893
28 January	1,200	1.302	1,562				2,750	3,455
31 January				1,500	1.256	1,884	1,250	1,571

(c)   The LIFO method for costing issues **will not** always mean that inventory is physically issued on a rotating basis so that the last inventory in is the first inventory issued.

7   GLOBE LTD

(a)   A – FIFO

(b)   Inventory record card

Date	Receipts			Issues			Balance	
	Tonnes	Cost per tonne (£)	Total cost (£)	Tonnes	Cost per tonne (£)	Total cost (£)	Tonnes	Total cost (£)
Balance as at 27 March							1,200	14,400
28 March	800	12.50	10,000				2,000	24,400
29 March				820	12.00	9,840	1,180	14,560
30 March	800	12.25	9,800				1,980	24,360
31 March				900	12.29	11,060	1,080	13,300

Working:

Issue on 31st March is made up of 380 @ 12 and 520 @12.50

8   A – FIFO

9   A

When prices are rising, FIFO will give a higher valuation for closing inventory, because the closing inventory will consist of the most recently-purchased items. Higher closing inventory means lower cost of sales and higher profit.

10   (a)

	Cost £	Workings
AVCO issue	523	(400 + 600 + 420) ÷ (50 + 80 + 60) = 7.4737 70 × 7.4737 = 523
FIFO issue	550	400 + (20 × 7.50) = 550
LIFO issue	495	(60 × 7.00) + (10 × 7.50) = 495
AVCO balance	897	(400 + 600 + 420) − 523 = 897
FIFO balance	870	(400 + 600 + 420) − 550 = 870
LIFO balance	925	(400 + 600 + 420) − 495 = 925

(b)   D

JOURNAL ENTRIES

INVENTORY

11   C

Materials inventory account

	£000s		£000s
Opening inventory	15	Issued to production	165
Payables for purchases	176	Returned to suppliers	8
Returned to stores	9	Written off	4
		Closing balance (balancing item)	23
	___		___
	200		200
	___		___

12

(a)   Return of 20 flap straps, costed at £50 each, from Maintenance to Stores

	Code	£
Debit	4000	1,000
Credit	5000	1,000

(b) **Payment to supplier for 15 padded steering wheels. These cost £75 each and were purchased on 30 day credit terms**

	Code	£
Debit	3000	1,125
Credit	2000	1,125

(c) **Payment on receipt of a delivery of fuel costing £1,200**

	Code	£
Debit	4000	1,200
Credit	2000	1,200

(d) **Issue of 300 litres of fuel at £1.23 to the short haul department**

	Code	£
Debit	8000	369
Credit	4000	369

13 B

Indirect materials are overhead costs so debit production overhead. An issue of materials is a credit from the material control account.

LABOUR

14

Date	Code	Dr £	Cr £
6 May	5000	1,650	
6 May	4000		1,650
11 May	6000	5,750	
11 May	4000		5,750
13 May	3022	5,100	
13 May	4000		5,100
15 May (Note)	3021	5,800	
15 May	4000		5,800

Note: In practice we would need to know the reason for the overtime to decide whether to treat it as direct or indirect. This question follows the treatment in the sample assessment.

15 **(a)** **The wages control account entries**

Wages control account

	£		£
Bank (net wages/salaries)	10,000	Maintenance (direct labour)	7,000
HMRC (income tax and NIC)	2,000	Maintenance overheads	4,000
Pension contribution	1,000	Maintenance administration	2,000
	13,000		**13,000**

(b) **The total payroll cost charged to the various cost accounts of the business**

Date	Code	Debit	Credit
30 November	8200		7,000
30 November	6200	7,000	
30 November	8200		4,000
30 November	6400	4,000	
30 November	8200		2,000
30 November	6600	2,000	

16

(a) **Payment of driver wages for the week amounting to 490 hours at £15.50 per hour**

	Code	£
Debit	6000	7,595
Credit	1000	7,595

(b) **Drivers worked 20 hours of overtime at time and a half at the specific request of a customer. How would the overtime premium be recorded in the accounts?**

	Code	£
Debit	8000	155
Credit	6000	155

(c) **The stores supervisor monthly salary of £2,000**

	Code	£
Debit	9000	2,000
Credit	6000	2,000

(d) **Drivers worked 10 hours of overtime at time and a half due to general work pressures. How would the overtime premium be recorded in the accounts?**

	Code	£
Debit	9000	77.50
Credit	6000	77.50

OVERHEADS

17   D

Over-absorbed overheads increase profit, and so are recorded as a credit entry in either an over-absorbed overhead account or directly as a credit in the income statement. The matching debit entry could be either in the WIP account or the production overhead control account, depending on the costing system used.

18   C

Wages control		Overhead control	
Indirect labour × (overheads)		Indirect labour × (wages)	

LABOUR COSTS

LABOUR

19   CARTCYLE LTD

Employee's weekly timesheet for week ending 7 December

Employee:		A. Man		Profit centre:		Wood finishing	
Employee number:		C812		**Basic pay per hour:**		£8.00	
	Hours spent on production	*Hours worked on indirect work*	*Notes*		*Basic pay £*	*Overtime premium £*	*Total pay £*
Monday	6	2	10am – 12am cleaning of machinery		64	8	72
Tuesday	2	4	9am – 1pm customer care course		48	0	48
Wednesday	8				64	8	72
Thursday	6				48	0	48
Friday	6	1	3 – 4pm health and safety training		56	4	60
Saturday	6				48	24	72
Sunday	3				24	24	48
Total	**37**	**7**			352	68	420

Alternative

Sunday	3				0	48	48
Total	**37**	**7**			328	92	420

20 **(a)**

	Units
Actual production	5,400,000
Standard production (5,000 hours at 800 units)	(4,000,000)
Excess production	1,400,000
Bonus %	$\dfrac{25\% \times 1,400,000}{4,000.000} = 8.75\%$
Group bonus rate per hour	0.0875 × £10 = £0.875
Total group bonus	5,000 hours at £0.875 = £4,375

(b)

Basic pay 44 hours at £9.60 =	£422.40
Bonus pay 44 hours at £0.875 =	£38.50
	_____
Total pay	£460.90

21 GRAPES

Employee's weekly timesheet for week ending 31 January

Employee:	Olivia Michael		Profit centre:		Moulding Department
Employee number:	P450		Basic pay per hour:		£10.00

	Hours spent in work	Hours worked on indirect work	Notes	Basic pay £	Overtime premium £	Total pay £
Monday	8	3	10am – 1pm cleaning moulds	80	5	85.00
Tuesday	7	4	9am – 1pm fire training	70	0	70.00
Wednesday	8			80	5	85.00
Thursday	7	1		70	0	70.00
Friday	7	1	3 – 4pm annual appraisal	70	0	70.00
Saturday	3			30	7.50	37.50
Total	**40**	**9**		400	17.50	417.50

Labour cost account

	£		£
Bank	417.50	Production	310
		Production Overheads	107.50

Production is direct labour only therefore basic hours less time spent on non-production activities:

$(40 - 9) \times £10 = £310$

Production overheads are the indirect costs therefore the cost is:

$£17.50 + (9 \times £10) = £107.50$

22 (a) Complete the gaps in the table below to calculate the total labour cost for the mechanics.

Labour cost	Hours	£
Basic pay	620	$620 \times 15 = 9{,}300$
Overtime rate 1	36	$36 \times (15 \times 1.3) = 702$
Overtime rate 2	20	$20 \times (15 \times 1.5) = 450$
Total cost before bonus		10,452
Bonus payment		$(5 + 3) \times 15 \times 0.75 = 90$
Total cost including bonus		10,542

(b) Calculate the direct labour cost per mechanic for May

$(620 + 36 + 20) \times 15 = £10{,}140/4 = £2{,}535$

(c) Complete the following sentence.

The total pay, including bonus, for each mechanic for June (to TWO decimal places) was:

$£10{,}542/4 = £2{,}635.50$

and of this total, the bonus payable to each team member (to TWO decimal places) was:

$90/4 = £22.50$

23 C

Product	Quantity	Standard time per item (hours)	Total Standard time (hours)
Buckles	50	0.2	10
Press studs	200	0.06	12
Belts	100	0.1	10
Buttons	10	0.7	7
			39

39 hours × £8 per hour = £312

24 **(a)** **Complete the gaps in the table below to calculate the total labour cost for the team in May**

Labour cost	Hours	£	Working
Basic pay	500	7,500	500 × 15
Overtime rate 1	50	1,125	50 × (15 × 1.5)
Overtime rate 2	20	600	20 × (15 × 2)
Total cost before bonus	570	9,225	
Bonus		750	500 × 15 × 0.1
Total cost including bonus		9,975	

(b) **Calculate the total labour cost of painting a pole in May:**

£9,975 ÷ 3,500 = 2.85

(c) **Complete the following sentences:**

The basic pay and overtime for each member of the team in May was £9,225 ÷ 5 = £1,845

The bonus payable to each team member was £750 ÷ 5 = £150

25 **(a)**

Total basic pay (£)	10,800 × 9 = £97,200
Total overtime premium (£)	2,450 × 5.50 = £13,475
Hours saved (hours)	400
Bonus (£)	400 × 9 × 0.35 = £1,260
Total direct labour cost (£)	£111,935

(b)

Equivalent units	Completed 300
	CWIP 200 × 0.75 150
	———
	EU 450
Bonus (£)	0

ACCOUNTING FOR OVERHEADS

OVERHEAD ALLOCATION AND APPORTIONMENT

26   D

Cost apportionment is concerned with sharing costs according to benefit received.

27   CARTCYLE LTD

	Basis of apportionment	Wood cutting £	Wood finishing £	Maintenance £	Stores £	General Admin £	Totals £
Depreciation of plant and equipment	CA of plant and equipment	1,013,229	434,241	–	–	–	1,447,470
Power for production machinery	Production machinery power usage (KwH)	772,200	514,800	–	–	–	1,287,000
Rent and rates	Floor space	–	–	94,050	56,430	37,620	188,100
Light and heat	Floor space	–	–	20,790	12,474	8,316	41,580
Indirect labour	Allocated	–	–	182,070	64,890	432,180	679,140
Totals		**1,785,429**	**949,041**	**296,910**	**133,794**	**478,116**	**3,643,290**
Reapportion Maintenance		207,837	89,073	(296,910)			
Reapportion Stores		86,966	46,828		(133,794)		
Reapportion General Admin		239,058	239,058			(478,116)	
Total overheads to production centres		2,319,290	1,324,000				3,643,290

28 AQUARIUS LTD

(a)

Overhead	Basis
Depreciation of plant and equipment	Carrying value of plant and equipment
Power for production machinery	Production machinery power usage
Rent and rates	Floor space
Light and heat	Floor space

(b)

	Basis of apportionment	Assembly £	Finishing £	Maintenance £	Stores £	Admin £	Totals £
Depreciation of plant and equipment	CA of plant and equipment	420,000	280,000	–	–	–	700,000
Power for production machinery	Production machinery power usage (KwH)	403,000	217,000	–	–	–	620,000
Rent and rates	Floor space	–	–	48,000	32,000	20,000	100,000
Light and heat	Floor space	–	–	9,600	6,400	4,000	20,000
Indirect labour	Allocated	–	–	102,000	40,000	240,000	382,000
Totals		**823,000**	**497,000**	**159,600**	**78,400**	**264,000**	**1,822,000**
Reapportion Admin		88,000	88,000	52,800	35,200	–264,000	
Reapportion Stores		56,800	34,080	22,720	–113,600		
Reapportion Maintenance		176,340	58,780	–235,120			
Total overheads to production centres		1,144,140	677,860				1,822,000

(c)   **Complete the following sentences by inserting the correct values.**

The fixed element of the quality control costs that will be apportioned to the Assembly department is:

£150,000 × 35% ÷ 100 × 47 = £24,675

The variable element of the quality control costs that will be apportioned to the Finishing department is:

£150,000 × 65% ÷ 100 × 62 = £60,450

29   F4L

	Basis of apportionment	Scheduled services	Charter flights	Aircraft maintenance and repairs	Fuel and parts store	General Admin £	Totals £
		£000	£000	£000	£000	£000	£000
Depreciation of aircraft	CA of aircraft	21,840	14,560	–	–	–	36,400
Aviation fuel and other variables	Planned number of miles flown	23,210	18,990	–	–	–	42,200
Pilots and aircrew salaries	Allocated	5,250	4,709	–	–	–	9,959
Rent and rates and other premises costs	Floor space	–	–	6,300	3,780	2,520	12,600
Indirect labour	Allocated	–	–	9,600	3,200	7,800	20,600
Totals		**50,300**	**38,259**	**15,900**	**6,980**	**10,320**	**121,759**
Reapportion Maintenance and repairs		9,540	6,360	(15,900)			
Reapportion fuel and parts store		3,839	3,141		(6,980)		
Reapportion General Admin		5,160	5,160			(10,320)	
Total overheads to profit centres		68,839	52,920				121,759

30   PREMIER LABELS LTD

	Basis of apportionment	Plastics Moulding	Labelling	Stores	Equipment Maintenance	Totals
Heat and lighting fixed cost	Allocated	6,000	6,000	6,000	6,000	24,000
Heat and lighting variable cost	Square meters occupied	19,200	10,800	4,800	1,200	36,000
Power for machinery	Percentages	19,600	8,400	–	–	28,000
Supervision	Direct labour cost	50,000	70,000	–	–	120,000
Stores wages	Allocated	–	–	72,000	–	72,000
Equipment maintenance salaries	Allocated	–	–	–	188,200	188,200
Depreciation of non-current assets	CA of non-current assets	48,000	24,000	9,000	3,000	84,000
Other overhead costs	Percentages	76,800	25,600	12,800	12,800	128,000
Totals		**219,600**	**144,800**	**104,600**	**211,200**	**680,200**
Reapportion Maintenance		70,400	70,400	70,400	(211,200)	
Reapportion Stores		130,200	44,800	(175,000)		
Total overheads to profit centres		420,200	260,000			680,200

OVERHEAD ABSORPTION

31   C

An absorption rate is used to determine the full cost of a product or service. Answer A describes overhead allocation and apportionment. Absorption does not control overheads, so answer D is not correct.

32   (a)   OAR = 586,792/9,464 = £62

The correct answer is A

(b)   Absorbed = 62 × 9,745 = £604,190

The correct answer is C

(c)   Over absorption = 604,190 – 568,631 = £35,559 over absorbed

The correct answer is A

33 **(a)** Assembly = 155,000/2,000 = £77.50 and Finishing = 105,000/1,750 = £60

The correct answer is B

(b) Assembly = 155,000/12,500 = £12.40 and Finishing = 105,000/8,750 = £12

The correct answer is D

(c) Absorbed overhead = 1,750 × 90% hours × £60 = £94,500

Therefore **£24,500 under** absorbed

34 **(a)** Moulding = 36,000/18,000 = £2 and Painting = 39,000/13,000 = £3

The correct answer is D

(b) Moulding = £2 × 17,500 = £35,000 and Painting = £3 × 13,500 = £40,500

The correct answer is A

(c) Moulding = 35,000 − 37,500 = £2,500 under absorbed and Painting = 40,500 − 40,000 = 500 over absorbed.

The correct answer is B

35 **(a)** Mixing = 64,800/10,000 = £6.48 and Bagging = 70,200/2,340 = £30.00

The correct answer is A

(b) Mixing = £6.48 × 9,000 = £58,320 and Bagging = £30.00 × 2,120 = £63,600

The correct answer is C

(c) Mixing = 58,320 − 67,500 = £9,180 under absorbed and Bagging = 63,600 − 75,600 = £12,000 under absorbed.

The correct answer is B

(d) Complete the following sentence

An under absorption of overheads will be **debited** to the Profit and Loss account. This will **increase** expenses and will **decrease** profit.

36 **A**

Under or over-absorption is determined by comparing the actual overhead expenditure with the overhead absorbed.

37 **D**

Fixed production overheads are over-absorbed when actual expenditure is less than budget and/or actual production volume is higher than budget.

ACTIVITY BASED COSTING

38 **D**

Statement (1) provides a definition of a cost driver. Cost drivers for long-term variable overhead costs will be the volume of a particular activity to which the cost driver relates, so Statement (2) is correct. Statement (3) is also correct. In traditional absorption costing, standard high-volume products receive a higher amount of overhead costs than with ABC. ABC allows for the unusually high costs of support activities for low-volume products (such as relatively higher set-up costs, order processing costs and so on).

39 **A**

40 **(a)** **C**

$$\text{Overhead absorption rate} = \frac{\text{Total overhead cost}}{\text{Total number of direct labour hours}}$$

Total overhead cost = 90,000 + 150,000 + 180,000 = £420,000

Total direct labour hours = (5 × 1,200) + (5 × 10,800) = 60,000 direct labour hours

Overhead absorption rate = £420,000 ÷ 60,000 direct labour hours

Overhead absorption rate = £7.00 per labour hour.

Alpha uses 5 direct labour hours per unit so will have an overhead cost per unit of 5 hours × £7.00 per hour = £35.00

(b) **C**

The overhead cost per unit for each unit of product Beta will be the same as product Alpha, as both products use the same number of labour hours (5 hours.)

(c) **D**

	Labour related	Purchasing related	Set-up related
Costs	£90,000	£150,000	£180,000
Consumption of activities (cost drivers)	60,000 labour hours	150 purchase orders	100 set-ups
Cost per unit of cost driver	£1.50 per labour hour	£1,000 per purchase order	£1,800 per set-up
Costs per product			
Product Alpha:	£1.50 × 6,000 labour hours = £9,000	£1,000 × 70 purchase orders = £70,000	£1,800 × 40 set-ups = £72,000
Product Beta:	£1.50 × 54,000 labour hours = £81,000	£1,000 × 80 purchase orders = £80,000	£1,800 × 60 set-ups = £108,000

Total overhead cost for Alpha = £9,000 + £70,000 + £72,000 = £151,000. Spread over 1,200 units, this represents a cost per unit of £125.83

(d) **B**

Total overhead cost for Beta = £81,000 + £80,000 + £108,000 = £269,000. Spread over 10,800 units, this represents a cost per unit of £24.91

41   C

Cost pool = £84,000

Cost driver = number of set-ups

Set ups A = 40,000 ÷ 2,000 = 20

Set ups B = 40,000 ÷ 5,000 = 8

Total set-ups 20 + 8 = 28

Rate per set up =£84,000 ÷ 28 = £3,000 per set-up

Cost for B = £3,000 × 8 set-ups = £24,000

Per unit = £24,000/40,000 = £0.60.

42   DOG

Workings:

Machine department

Total cost £20,800

Total machine hours = (8 × 240) + (6 × 200) + (4 × 160) + (6 × 240) = 5,200 hours

Cost per hour = £20,800 ÷ 5,200 hours = £4.00 per hour

W = £4 × 8hr × 240 units = £7,680

X = £4 × 6hr × 200 units = £4,800

Y = £4 × 4hr × 160 units = £2,560

Z = £4 × 6hr × 240 units = £5,760

Set up

Total cost £10,500

Total production runs = (240 + 200 + 160 + 240) ÷ 40 = 21 runs

Cost per run = £10,500 ÷ 21 = £500 per run

W = £500 × (240 ÷ 40) = £3,000

X = £500 × (200 ÷ 40) = £2,500

Y = £500 × (160 ÷ 40) = £2,000

Z = £500 × (240 ÷ 40) = £3,000

Stores receiving

Total cost £7,200

Total requisitions raised = 40 × 4 = 160

Cost per requisition = £7,200 ÷ 160 = £45 per requisition

W = £45 × 40 = £1,800

X = £45 × 40 = £1,800

Y = £45 × 40 = £1,800

Z = £45 × 40 = £1,800

Total costs	W	X	Y	Z
	£	£	£	£
Direct materials	19,200	20,000	9,600	28,800
Direct labour	13,440	8,400	4,480	10,080
Machine department costs	7,680	4,800	2,560	5,760
Set up costs	3,000	2,500	2,000	3,000
Stores receiving	1,800	1,800	1,800	1,800
Total cost	45,120	37,500	20,440	49,440
Cost per unit	188.00	187.50	127.75	206.00

ACTIVITY EFFECTS

COST BEHAVIOURS

43 C

	£
Total cost of 18,500 hours	251,750
Total cost of 17,000 hours	246,500
Variable cost of 1,500 hours	5,250

Variable cost per machine hour = £5,250/1,500 machine hours = £3.50.

	£
Total cost of 17,000 hours	246,500
Less variable cost of 17,000 hours (× £3.50)	59,500
Balance = fixed costs	187,000

44 A

	Cost per unit (£) (125 units)	Cost per unit (£) (180 units)
T1	8.00	7.00
T2	14.00	14.00
T3	19.80	15.70
T4	25.80	25.80

Cost types T2 and T4 are variable and T1 and T3 are semi-variable.

45

	Description
Variable cost	Increase in total as volume increases
Fixed cost	Decreases per unit as volume increases
Stepped cost	Fixed for a certain volume range only
Semi-variable cost	Made up of fixed and variable costs

46   Graph 1 C; Graph 2 D

47   **C**

48   A **profit** centre manager will be sent overall performance reports to monitor revenues.

Investment centre managers will be sent reports detailing the returns on capital employed.

A **cost** centre manager will be sent details about amounts spent on maintaining machinery.

49   **TRUCK TRANSPORT**

Cost	Classification (tick correct answer)				Total cost at 5,000 miles (£)
	Variable	Semi-variable	Fixed	Stepped fixed	
Cost 1				✓	27,000
Cost 2	✓				35,000
Cost 3			✓		31,500
Cost 4		✓			39,000

Working for Cost 4

Total cost at lowest level = 1,500 × £12.00 = £18,000

Total cost at highest level = 6,000 × £7.50 = £45,000

VC per unit = (£45,000 − £18,000) / (6,000 − 1,500) = £6.00

Total fixed cost = £45,000 − (6,000 × £6.00) = £9,000

Total cost at 5,000 units = £9,000 + (5,000 × £6.00) = £39,000

50 CARTCYCLE LTD

Batches produced and sold	2,160	2,700	3,600
	£	£	£
Sales revenue	64,800	81,000	108,000
Variable costs:			
• Direct materials	9,720	12,150	16,200
• Direct labour	22,680	28,350	37,800
• Overheads	12,960	16,200	21,600
Semi-variable costs:	6,804		
• Variable element		5,400	7,200
• Fixed element		2,484	2,484
Total cost	52,164	64,584	85,284
Total profit	12,636	16,416	22,716
Profit per batch (to 2 decimal places)	5.85	6.08	6.31

51 CHARTER FLIGHTS

Likely miles	5,000	6,000	7,000
	£000	£000	£000
Sale revenue	2,500	2,950	3,400
Variable/semi-variable costs:			
• Aviation fuel	400	480	560
• Landing and servicing fees	850	900	950
• Other variable overheads	135	162	189
Fixed costs:			
• Wages and salaries	420	420	420
• Other fixed overheads	625	625	625
Total cost	2430	2,587	2,744
Total profit	70	363	656
Profit per mile flown (2 d.p.) £	14.00	60.50	93.71

52 **(a)** **£24,000 ÷ 800 = £30**

(b) VC = £3,600 + £8,400 + £1,800 = £13,800

VC per unit = £13,800 ÷ 800 = £17.25

SV VC per unit = (£4,920 − £2,520) ÷ (1,600 − 800) = £3.00

Total VC per unit = **£20.25**

(c) FC = £2,520 − (800 × 3) = £120

FC per unit = £120 ÷ 1,200 = **£0.10**

(d) Total cost = (£20.25 × 1,500) + 120 = £30,495

Total cost per unit = £30,495 ÷ 1,500 = **£20.33**

(e) Contribution per unit = £30 − £20.25 = £9.75

Total contribution = £9.75 × 1,500 = £14,625

Total profit = £14,625 − £120 = £14,505

Profit per unit = £14,505 ÷ 1,500 = **£9.67**

SEGMENTAL REPORTING

53 **(a)**

	Route S	Route SE	Route SW
Contract miles	3,000	3,000 × 80% = 2,400	3,000 × 1.20 = 3,600
Revenue and costs			
Revenue (£000s)	3,000 × £150 = £450,000 **450**	2,400 × £150 × 1.1 = 396,000 **396**	3,600 × £150 × 90% = 486,000 **486**
Variable costs (£000s)	3,000 × £80 £240,000 **240**	2,400 × £85 = £204,000 **204**	3,600 × £80 × 93.75% = £270,000 **270**
Contribution (£000)	450 − 240 = **210**	396 − 204 = **192**	486 − 270 = **216**
Fixed costs (£000)	80	120	200
Profit (£000s)	130	72	16

(b) Looking at the information in part (a), indicate how you should react to the following scenario by ticking yes or no in the table.

Scenario	Yes	No
You are asked to change the variable cost figure to increase profit. There is no evidence to support the change in cost. Do you do this?		✓
You discover an error that will significantly impact the profit for one of the routes. Do you report this to your manager?	✓	
While completing the forecast you wonder why the different routes are charged different rates per mile. Do you ask your manager to explain?	✓	
A friend of the family works for a competitor and would like to see your forecast calculations. Do you let them see?		✓

54   INDIA LTD

	Rose (£)	Tulip (£)	Buttercup (£)	Total (£)
Selling price per unit	50.00	120.00	80.00	
Less: Variable costs per units				
Direct material	10.00	24.00	16.00	
Direct labour	13.00	44.00	21.00	
Contribution per unit	27.00	52.00	43.00	
Sales volume (units)	1,000	200	500	
Total contribution	27,000	10,400	21,500	58,900
Less: fixed costs				52,000
Budgeted profit				6,900

55   SPORT SHIRT LTD

(a)

	New £	Existing £	Total £
Sales revenue	24,000	60,000	
Less: variable costs			
Direct materials	7,500	12,000	
Direct labour	2,500	7,500	
Total contribution	14,000	40,500	54,500
Less: fixed costs			33,750
Budgeted profit			20,750

(b)   B

SHORT TERM DECISION MAKING

COST VOLUME PROFIT ANALYSIS

56 Choose the correct description for each of the following:

Term
Contribution
Breakeven point
Margin of safety

Description
Selling price less variable costs
Sales units where is no profit or loss
Excess of actual sales over breakeven sales

57 **(a)** £7.20 × 9,000 = £64,800

(b)

$$\frac{64,800}{41.40 - 27} = 4,500 \text{ units}$$

(c)

Units of MR 13 sold	9,000
Margin of safety (units)	9,000 – 4,500 = 4,500 units
Margin of safety percentage	$\dfrac{9,000 - 4,500}{9,000} \times 100 = 50\%$

(d) The correct answer is **A** – an increase in selling price means that contribution per unit increases therefore fewer units have to be made to cover the fixed costs. If BEP is lower than the margin of safety is higher.

(e)

	Product MR13
Number of units to be sold to meet target profit	$\dfrac{£36,000 + £64,800}{£14.40} = 7,000 \text{ units}$
Revised margin of safety (%)	$\dfrac{9,000 - 7,000}{9,000} \times 100 = 22.22\%$
Revised margin of safety in sales revenue (£)	2,000 × £41.40 = £82,800

58 **(a)** Contribution = £0.80 – £0.30 = £0.50

£312,500 ÷ £0.50 × £0.80 = £500,000

OR using the PV ratio $\dfrac{£312,500}{£0.50/£0.80} = £500,000$

(b) Using the PV ratio = $\dfrac{£312,500 + £200,000}{£0.50/£0.80} = £820,000$

(c) (i) £875,000 – £500,000 = £375,000

(ii) £375,000/£500,000 × 100 = 75%

59 **(a)**

	A (£)	B (£)	Total (£)
Selling price per unit	1.50	1.20	
Less: variable costs per unit			
Direct materials	0.20	0.25	
Direct labour	0.12	0.14	
Variable overheads	0.15	0.19	
Contribution per unit	1.03	0.62	
Sales volume (units)	300,000	500,000	
Total contribution	309,000	310,000	619,000
Less: fixed costs			264,020
Budgeted profit or loss			354,980

(b)

Product	A	B
Fixed costs (£)	158,620	105,400
Unit contribution (£)	1.03	0.62
Break-even sales (units)	154,000	170,000
Forecast sales (units)	250,000	400,000
Margin of safety (units)	96,000	230,000
Margin of safety (%)	38.40	57.50

(c)

Product A		Product B		✓

60 **(a)**

Likely miles	10,000	12,000	14,000
	£	£	£
Sales revenue	100,000	120,000	140,000
Variable costs:			
• Fuel	8,000	9,600	11,200
• Drivers' wages and associated costs	5,000	6,000	7,000
• Overheads	6,000	7,200	8,400
Fixed costs:			
• Indirect labour	10,600	10,600	10,600
• Overheads	25,850	25,850	25,850
Total cost	55,450	59,250	63,050
Total profit	44,550	60,750	76,950
Profit per mile	4.455	5.063	5.496

(b)

Forecast number of miles		12,000	14,000
Sales revenue	£	120,000	140,000
Fixed costs	£	36,450	
Contribution	£	97,200	
Contribution per mile	£	8.10	
Break-even number of miles	Miles	4,500	
Break-even sales revenue	£	45,000	
Margin of safety in number of miles	Miles	7,500	9,500
Margin of safety in sales revenue	£	75,000	95,000
Margin of safety	%	62.50	67.86

61 Line A is total revenue

Line B is total costs

Line C is total variable costs

Line D is fixed costs

62 (a) Calculate the breakeven volume of 0.8m poles:

Contribution per unit = 10 − [(75 + 200 + 250) ÷ 150] = £6.50

BEP = £325 ÷ £6.50 = 50 units

(b) Calculate the breakeven sales revenue of 0.8m poles

50 units × £10 = £500

(c) How many 2.8m poles must Jump sell to reach its target profit of £2,400

Target profit = (£450 + £2,400) ÷ (£1,500 ÷ 50) = 95 poles

(d) Calculate the margin of safety of the 2.8m pole (in poles)

Contribution per pole = (£1,500 ÷ 50) = £30

BEP = £450 ÷ £30 = 15 poles

Target sales = (£450 + £2,400) ÷ £30 = 95 poles

Margin of safety = 95 − 15 = 80 poles

LIMITING FACTOR ANALYSIS

63   D

Material required to meet maximum demand:

$(6,000 \times 3.25) + (8,000 \times 4.75) =$ 57,500 litres

Material available: 50,000 litres

∴ Material is a limiting factor

Labour required to meet maximum demand:

$(6,000 \times 5) + (8,000 \times 4) =$ 62,000 hours

Labour available: 60,000 hours

∴ Labour is a limiting factor

64   (a)

	Apple (£)	Banana (£)	Total (£)
Selling price per bar	3.00	2.40	
Less: variable costs per unit			
Direct materials	0.40	0.50	
Direct labour	0.24	0.28	
Variable overheads	0.30	0.38	
Contribution per unit	2.06	1.24	
Sales volume (bars)	75,000	125,000	
Total contribution	154,500	155,000	309,500
Less: fixed costs			150,000
Budgeted profit or loss			159,500

(b)

Product	Apple bars	Banana bars	Total
Contribution/unit (£)	2.06	1.24	
Machine hours/unit	0.40	0.16	
Contribution/machine hour (£)	5.15	7.75	
Product ranking	2	1	
Machine hours available			35,000
Machine hours allocated to: Product: Banana Product: Apple	15,000	20,000	
Units made	37,500	125,000	
Total contribution	77,250	155,000	232,250
Less: fixed costs (£)			150,000
Profit/loss made (£)			82,250

65 **(a)**

Product	Squeakers	Hooters	Total
Contribution per unit (£)	20/80 = 0.25	24.5/70 = 0.35	
Contribution per machine hour (£)	20/40 = 0.50	24.5/17.5 = 1.40	
Ranking	2	1	
Total machine hours available			50,000
Machine hours allocated to	32,500	17,500	
Units made	32,500/(40/80) = 65,000	70,000	
Total contribution earned (£)	65,000 × 0.25 = 16,250	24,500	40,750
Less: fixed costs (£)			15,000
Forecast profit/loss made (£)			25,750

(b) Hooters should be selected as the first product to be made as it has the **highest contribution per machine hour**

66 **CPL**

Product	AB1	CD2	EF3	Total
Contribution/pack (£)	4.00	5.00	3.00	
Kgs of plant extract/pack	0.40	0.25	0.50	
Contribution/kg (£)	10	20	6	
Product ranking	2	1	3	
Kgs of plant extract available				6,000
Kgs allocated to each product	2,640	1,730	1,630	
Number of packs to produce	6,600	6,920	3,260	
Total contribution earned (£)	26,400	34,600	9,780	70,780
Less: Fixed costs (£)				30,780
Profit/loss made (£)				40,000

67 **(a)**

	Asparagus soup	Broccoli soup	
	p	p	
Selling price per can	60	50	
Less: variable costs per can			
Direct materials	7	6	
Direct labour	6	7	
Variable overheads	2	3	
Contribution per can	45	34	
	No of cans	No of cans	
Sales volume (cans)	1,200,000	1,800,000	
	£	£	Total (£)
Total contribution	540,000	612,000	1,152,000
Less: fixed costs			652,000
Budgeted profit or loss			500,000

(b)

Product	Asparagus soup	Broccoli soup	Total
Contribution/can (£)	0.45	0.34	
Machine hours/can	0.005	0.005	
Contribution/machine hour (£)	90	68	
Product ranking	1	2	
Machine hours available			12,000
Machine hours allocated to: Product: Asparagus Soup Product: Broccoli Soup	6,000	6,000	
Units made	1,200,000	1,200,000	
Total contribution	540,000	408,000	948,000
Less: fixed costs (£)			652,000
Profit/loss made (£)			296,000

TYPES OF COSTING SYSTEMS

JOB, BATCH AND SERVICE COSTING

68   C

	Job 812
	£
Direct materials	60
Direct labour	40
Direct expenses	20
Prime cost	120
Production overheads (£40 ÷ 8) × £16	80
Non-production overheads (0.6 × £120)	72
Total cost – Job 812	272

69   C

	£
Prime cost	6,840.00
Fixed overhead £300,000 ÷ 60,000 × 156	780.00
	7,620.00

Cost per unit = 7,620 ÷ 500 = **£15.24**

70   B

Average cost per occupied bed per day

$$= \frac{\text{Total cost}}{\text{Number of beds occupied}}$$

$$= \frac{£100,000 + £5,000 + £22,500}{6,450 \times 2} = £9.88$$

or £127,500/(200 × 2 + 30) × 30 = £9.88

71   C

A service is intangible and inventory cannot be held. Services generally have a high level of fixed costs and there are often difficulties in identifying a suitable cost unit.

PROCESS COSTING – LOSSES/GAINS

72   CARTCYCLE LTD

(a)

Description	Kg's	Unit cost £	Total cost £	Description	Kg's	Unit cost £	Total cost £
Material TR10	1,080	2.16	2,333	Normal loss	126	1.08	136
Material DG41	720	2.70	1,944	Output	2,300	8.316	19,127
Material IG11	720	1.10	792	Abnormal loss	94	8.316	782
Labour			5,760				
Overheads			9,216				
	2,520		20,045		2,520		20,045

(b)

	Debit	Credit
Abnormal loss		✓
Abnormal gain	✓	

73   D

Abnormal loss units are valued as one equivalent unit of cost, the same as units of good production. This cost is credited to the process account and debited to the abnormal loss account. The scrap value of abnormal loss is then credited to the abnormal loss account (with the matching debit to bank).

74   (a)   Complete the table below to show the total cost of the materials input into the process.

	£
Material CBB	910
Material BSS	560
Material SMA	360

(b)   Calculate the total labour cost and total overhead cost

Total labour cost £	Total overhead cost £
2,560	3,840

(c)   Calculate the total quantity and value of inputs into the process

Total quantity (kg)	Total cost £
1,700	8,230

(d)   Calculate the total scrap value of the normal loss

Value of scrap £
(1,700 × 2%) × 0.50 = £17

(e)   Calculate the cost per kilogram of output assuming a normal loss of 2% of input. State your answer to 2 decimal places.

Cost per kilogram £
(£8,230 – £17) ÷ (1,700 – 34) = £4.93

(f)   If output is 1,600 calculate if there has been an abnormal loss or gain, the quantity of the loss or gain and the value of the loss

Abnormal loss or gain	Quantity of loss or gain (kg)	Value of loss or gain
Abnormal loss	1,700 – 1,600 – 34 = 66	66 × £4.93 = £325

75   GRAPE LTD

Description	Units	Unit cost £	Total cost £	Description	Units	Unit cost £	Total cost £
Input – Statues	300	11.25	3,375	Normal loss	30	5.00	150
Materials – Glaze			500	Output	290	49.35	14,312
Labour			5,760				
Overheads			3,840				
Abnormal gain	20	49.35	987				
	320		14,462		320		14,462

76   (a)

$$\frac{(500 \times 17.20) + (280 \times 10.50) + (86 \times 32) - (500 \times 5\% \times 1.68)}{500 - (500 \times 5\%)} = £30$$

(b)

Description	Litres	Cost per litre £	Total cost £	Description	Litres	Cost per litre £	Total cost £
Materials	500	17.20	8,600	Output	490	30.00	14,700
Labour			2,940	Normal loss	25	1.68	42
Overheads			2,752				
Abnormal gain	15	30.00	450				
	515		14,742		515		14,742

PROCESS COSTING – EQUIVALENT UNITS

77 Statement of EU

	Materials	Conversion
Completed	5,000	5,000
CWIP	600	300
TOTAL EU	5,600	5,300
Costs		
Period costs	56,000	26,500
		10,600
TOTAL COSTS	56,000	37,100
Cost per EU	10.00	7.00

78 Statement of EU

	Materials	Conversion
Completed	9,000	9,000
CWIP	3,500	2,625
TOTAL EU	12,500	11,625
Costs		
Period costs	18,750	12,415
		16,415
TOTAL COSTS	18,750	28,830
Cost per EU	1.50	2.48

Valuation of output

Completed units = 9,000 × (1.50 + 2.48) = **£35,820**

Closing WIP = (3,500 × 1.50) + (2,625 × 2.48) = **£11,760**

79 B

	Labour
Completed (7,000 × 100%)	7,000
CWIP (1,200 × 50%)	600
TOTAL EU	7,600
Costs	
Period costs	3,800
TOTAL COSTS	3,800
Cost per EU	0.50

80

	Material	Conversion
EU to complete OWIP	300 × (100 − 80)% = 60	300 × (100 − 60)% = 120

81

	Material	Conversion
EU to complete OWIP	200 × (100 − 100)% = 0	200 × (100 − 45)% = 110

82

(a)

	Material	Conversion
Cost per EU £	3.10	5.90

Working

OWIP + Inputs = Output + CWIP

300 + 700 = 800 + 200

Equivalent units	Material	Conversion
OWIP to complete	300 × 0% = 0	300 × 40% = 120
Completed output	500 × 100% = 500	500 × 100% = 500
CWIP	200 × 100% = 200	200 × 70% = 140
Total EU	700	760
Costs		
Period cost only £	2,170	4,484
Cost per EU	£2,170 ÷ 700 EU = £3.10	£4,484 ÷ 760 = £5.90

(b)

	Completed output	CWIP
Value £	9,058	1,446

Completed output

OWIP b/f = £1,150 + £2,700	£3,850
Cost to complete OWIP = 120 EU × £5.90	£708
Completed output = 500 EU × (£3.10 + £5.90)	£4,500
	£9,058
Closing WIP = 200 EU × £3.10 + 140 EU × £5.90	£1,446

83

(a)

	Material	Conversion
Cost per EU £	1.50	1.05

Working

OWIP + Inputs = Output + CWIP

2,000 + 7,000 = 8,000 + 1,000

Equivalent units	Material	Conversion
Completed output	8,000 × 100% = 8,000	8,000 × 100% = 8,000
CWIP	1,000 × 100% = 1,000	1,000 × 60% = 600
Total EU	9,000	8,600

Costs

	Material	Conversion
OWIP b/f	4,000	1,950
Period cost £	9,500	7,080
Total £	13,500	9,030
Cost per EU	£13,500 ÷ 9,000 EU = £1.50	£9,030 ÷ 8,600 EU = £1.05

(b)

	Completed output	CWIP
Value £	20,400	2,130

Completed output = 8,000 EU × (£1.50 + £1.05)   £20,400

Closing WIP = 1,000 EU × £1.50 + 600 EU × £1.05   £2,130

ABSORPTION AND MARGINAL COSTING

84 B

The marginal cost of a product is the additional cost of producing an extra unit and is therefore the sum of the variable costs. If the inventory increases over a year, absorption costing profit will be higher than marginal costing profit because an element of fixed cost will be carried forward in closing inventory to be charged against profit in a future period.

85 A

Total contribution will increase as sales volume increases, but the contribution per unit will be constant as long as the sales price and variable cost per unit are unchanged. Overhead is not absorbed into the product unit so there is no under/over absorption of overhead. Marginal costing *does* provide useful information for decision making because it highlights contribution, which is a relevant cash flow for decision-making purposes.

86 The cost per mile under:

(a) **Marginal costing**

Fuel and other variable overheads	£ per mile
Total variable cost per mile £9,200/4,600 miles	**2.00**

(b) **Absorption costing**

Fuel and other variable overheads	£ per mile
Total variable cost per mile £9,200/4,600 miles	2.00
Drivers' wages, pension and national insurance £3,220/4,600 miles	0.70
Fixed overheads £23,000/4,600 miles	5.00
Total absorption cost per mile	**7.70**

87 Marginal costing

	£000	£000
Sales		50,000
Opening inventory	0	
Production costs (7,560 + 17,640)	25,200	
Closing inventory (25,200/1,800 × 800)	−11,200	
Cost of sales		−14,000
Contribution		36,000
Fixed costs (3,600 + 2,010)		−5,610
Profit for the period		30,390

Absorption costing

	£000	£000
Sales		50,000
Opening inventory	0	
Production costs (7,560 + 17,640 + 3,600)	28,800	
Closing inventory (28,800/1,800 × 800)	−12,800	
Cost of sales		−16,000
Gross Profit		34,000
Non-production cost		−2,010
Profit for the period		31,990

88 (a) **Marginal costing**

	£	£
Sales (12 × 12,000)		144,000
Opening inventory (7 × 2,000)	14,000	
Production costs (7 × 15,000)	105,000	
Closing inventory (7 × 5,000)	−35,000	
Cost of sales		−84,000
Contribution		60,000
Fixed costs		−30,000
Profit for the period		30,000

(b) **£36,000**

Fixed cost per unit = £30,000 ÷ 15,000 = £2 per unit

Absorption costing profit = 30,000 − FC in opening inventory + FC in closing inventory

= 30,000 − (2 × 2,000) + (2 × 5,000) = £36,000

OR

Absorption costing profit		??
Change in inventory × OAR	(2,000 − 5,000) × £2	−£6,000
Marginal costing profit		£30,000

£30,000 + £6,000 = £36,000

89 **(a)**

	£
Selling price/unit	40
Prime cost/unit	(12)
Variable production cost/unit	(4)
Contribution/unit	24

(b)

	£
Selling price/unit	40
Marginal cost/unit	(16)
Fixed production cost/unit (£120,000/12,000 units)	(10)
Profit/unit	14

(c) Absorption costing

	£	£
Sales (40 × 10,000)		400,000
Opening inventory (26 × 500)	13,000	
Production costs (26 × 12,000)	312,000	
Closing inventory (26 × 2,500)	−65,000	
Cost of sales		−260,000
Gross Profit		140,000
Non-production costs		0
Profit for the period		140,000

(d) **£120,000**

Total contribution = £24 × 10,000 sales units = £240,000

Profit = total contribution − total fixed costs = £240,000 − £120,000 = £120,000

OR

Absorption costing profit		£140,000
Change in inventory	(500 − 2,500) × 10 =	−20,000
Marginal costing profit		£120,000

90   B

In an absorption costing system, the fixed cost per unit would be £3,000/15,000 units = £0.20 per unit.

By switching to absorption costing, in a period when inventory levels increase by 2,000 units, absorption costing profit would be higher by 2,000 units × fixed cost per unit, i.e. by 2,000 × £0.20 = £400.

Absorption costing profit = £23,000 + £400 = £23,400.

91   (a)   Calculate the estimated prime cost per batch of painted poles

£4,500 + £5,000 = £9,500

(b)   Calculate the estimated marginal production cost per batch of painted poles

£9,500 + £2,500 = £12,000

(c)   Calculate the estimated full absorption cost of one batch of painted poles

£12,000 + £1,750 = £13,750

(d)

	Tick
Variable costs	✓
Fixed costs	✓
Sales revenue	
Assets and liabilities	

BASIC VARIANCE ANALYSIS

VARIANCE ANALYSIS

92   D

93   AQUARIUS LTD

	Flexed budget	Actual	Variance	Favourable F or Adverse A
Volume sold	267,000	267,000		
	£000	£000	£000	
Sales revenue	2,136	2,409	273	F
Less costs:				
Direct materials	534	801	267	A
Direct labour	267	267	0	0
Fixed overheads	600	750	150	A
Profit from operations	735	591	144	A

94 GRAPE LTD

(a)

	Original budget	Flexed budget	Actual	Variance
Volume sold	20,000	28,800	28,800	
	£000	£000	£000	£000
Sales revenue	3,000	4,320	3,877	−443
Less costs:				
Direct materials	175	252	212	40
Direct labour	875	1,260	912	348
Variable overheads	445	641	448	193
Fixed overheads	300	300	325	−25
Profit from operations	1,205	1,867	1,980	113

(b)   C

(c)   C

95 GLOBE LTD

(a)

	Original budget	Flexed budget	Actual	Variance
Volume sold	4,000	5,000	5,000	
	£000	£000	£000	£000
Sales revenue	1,500	1,875	1,950	75
Less costs:				
Direct materials	36	45	45	0
Direct labour	176	220	182	38
Variable overheads	92	115	90	25
Profit from operations	1,196	1,495	1,633	138

(b)   B

(c)   D

The flexed budget has already taken account of the increase in units sold, offering a bulk discount should increase units sales but at a reduced price, increased competition from other companies could lead to a reduction in sales units and prices

LONG TERM DECISION MAKING

PAYBACK, NPV AND IRR

96

Appraisal method	Recommendation
Payback period	Reject as more than 3 years
Net present value	Accept as positive
Internal Rate of Return	Accept as greater than cost of capital
Overall	Accept as per most important investment criterion

97 **(a)** For the first investment Truck Transport should invest in option **1** as it has the **shortest payback period**

For the second investment Truck Transport should invest in option **4** as it has the **highest NPV**

(b)

Statement	True	False
Payback method uses profits from a project to determine the payback period		✓
If the IRR is less than the cost of capital for a project, then it should be undertaken		✓
The IRR method uses discounted cash flows	✓	
Projects with a negative NPV should be rejected	✓	

98 **(a)**

	Year 0 £000	Year 1 £000	Year 2 £000	Year 3 £000
Capital expenditure	−1,620			
Sales income		756	1,008	1,440
Operating costs		−216	−270	−342
Net cash flows	−1,620	540	738	1,098
PV factors	1.0000	0.8696	0.7561	0.6575
Discounted cash flows	−1,620	470	558	722
Net present value	130			

The net present value is **positive**

(b)

Year	Cash flow £000	Cumulative cash flow £000
0	(1,620)	(1,620)
1	540	(1,080)
2	738	(342)
3	1,098	756

The payback period is **2** years and **4** months.

Months = 342/1,098 × 12 = 3.7 months

99 **(a)**

	Year 0 £000	Year 1 £000	Year 2 £000	Year 3 £000
Capital expenditure	−1,200			
Sales income		530	570	710
Operating costs		−140	−160	−170
Net cash flows	−1,200	390	410	540
PV factors	1.0000	0.8696	0.7561	0.6575
Discounted cash flows	−1,200	339	310	355
Net present value	−196			

The net present value is **negative**

(b)

Year	Cash flow £000	Cumulative cash flow £000
0	(1,200)	(1,200)
1	390	(810)
2	410	(400)
3	540	140

The payback period is **2** years and **9** months.

Months = 400/540 × 12 = 8.9 months

100 (a)

	Year 0 £000	Year 1 £000	Year 2 £000	Year 3 £000
Capital expenditure	−500			
Sales income		280	330	370
Operating costs		−100	−120	−140
Net cash flows	−500	180	210	230
PV factors	1.0000	0.909	0.826	0.751
Discounted cash flows	−500	164	173	173
Net present value	10			

The net present value is **positive**

(b)   D

(c)

Year	Cash flow £000	Cumulative cash flow £000
0	(500)	(500)
1	180	(320)
2	210	(110)
3	230	120

The payback period is **2** years and **6** months.

Months = 110/230 × 12 = 5.7 months

101 Bartrum Ltd

Machine A

	Year 0 £000	Year 1 £000	Year 2 £000	Year 3 £000
Capital expenditure	−1,085			
Net cash flows	−1,085	−200	−200	−200
PV factors	1.0000	0.8696	0.7561	0.6575
Discounted cash flows	−1,085	−174	−151	−132
Net present cost	−1,542			

Machine B

	Year 0 £000	Year 1 £000	Year 2 £000	Year 3 £000
Capital expenditure	−1,200			
Net cash flows	−1,200	−150	−160	−170
PV factors	1.0000	0.8696	0.7561	0.6575
Discounted cash flows	−1,200	−130	−121	−112
Net present cost	−1,563			

Bartrum should invest in **Machine A**

102 Van type P

	Year 0 £000	Year 1 £000	Year 2 £000	Year 3 £000
Capital expenditure	−600			
Disposal				150
Net cash flows	−600	−275	−290	−165
PV factors	1.0000	0.8621	0.7432	0.6407
Discounted cash flows	−600	−237	−216	−106
Net present cost	−1,159			

Van type R

	Year 0 £000	Year 1 £000	Year 2 £000	Year 3 £000
Capital expenditure/disposal	−750			170
Net cash flows	−750	−345	−365	−220
PV factors	1.0000	0.8621	0.7432	0.6407
Discounted cash flows	−750	−297	−271	−141
Net present cost	−1,459			

CPL should invest in **Van type P**

103 (a) **No**

(b) **Yes**

(c) £ Nil

104

REPORT

To: The Chief Accountant

From: AAT student

Subject: Investment appraisal

Date: 3 December 20X2

The payback period of 2.4 years is *within* the company's policy of 3 years, and on this criterion the investment *should go* ahead.

The NPV is *negative* and on this criterion the investment *should not go* ahead.

The IRR, at 14%, is *below* the company's 16% cost of capital and on this criterion the investment *should not go* ahead.

Overall the investment *should not* proceed because the *NPV* is the dominant criterion.

---

105 **14%**

$$10 + \frac{£17,706}{(£17,706--£4,317)} \times (15-10) = 14\%$$

OR BY APPROXIMATION

NPV at 10% = £17,706

NPV at 15% = −£4,317

Change in discount rate = 5% and change in NPV = £22,023

Therefore 1% = £22,023/5 = £4,405

The NPV at 15% is −£4,317 therefore to get to a zero return the IRR is approximately 14%

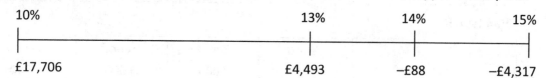

10%		13%	14%	15%
£17,706		£4,493	−£88	−£4,317

106 C

Year	Cash £	20%	PV £
0	(75,000)		(75,000)
1	25,000	0.833	20,825
2	25,000	0.694	17,350
3	25,000	0.579	14,475
4	25,000	0.482	12,050
5	25,000	0.402	10,050
			(250)

$$\text{IRR} = 15 + \frac{8,800}{8,800 - (250)} \times 5$$

$$\text{IRR} = 15 + \frac{8,800}{9,050} \times 5$$

IRR = 19.86% therefore **20%** to the nearest 1%

OR BY APPROXIMATION

NPV at 15% = £8,800

NPV at 20% = −£250

Change in discount rate = 5% and change in NPV = £9,050

Therefore 1% = £9,050 ÷ 5 = £1,810

The NPV at 20% is −£250 therefore the discount rate to the nearest 1% is 20%

Section 3

MOCK ASSESSMENT QUESTIONS

TASK 1   **(16 MARKS)**

Sarloue Ltd has the following information available for superfine oil S07:

Date purchased	Quantity (litres)	Cost per litre (£)	Total cost (£)
5 July	625	2.20	1,375
16 July	550	2.40	1,320
22 July	650	2.50	1,625

Calculate the cost of an issue of 600 litres on 20 July and the inventory balance at the end of the month (round to the nearest £).

	Cost (£)
AVCO issue	
AVCO balance	
FIFO issue	
FIFO balance	

TASK 2 (16 MARKS)

Put the correct entries into the Journal below to record the following FOUR accounting transactions:

1   Receipt of 700 litres of oil at £2.60 into inventory paying by cheque.

2   Issue of 450 litres of oil at £2.40 from inventory to production.

3   Receipt of 600 litres of oil at £2.35 into inventory paying on credit.

4   Return of £1,500 of oil from inventory to a supplier who had sold the oil on credit.

The account choices are:

Bank, Inventory, Trade payables' control, Inventory, Production

	Account	Dr (£)	Cr (£)
Transaction 1			
Transaction 2			
Transaction 3			
Transaction 4			

TASK 3 (12 MARKS)

Below is a weekly timesheet for one of Sarloue Ltd's employees, who is paid as follows:

- For a basic seven and a half hour shift every day from Monday to Friday – basic pay.

- For any overtime in excess of the basic seven and a half hours, on any day from Monday to Friday – the extra hours are paid at time-and-a-half.

- For any hours worked on Saturday or Sunday – paid at double time.

Complete the columns headed Basic pay, Overtime premium and Total pay:

(**Notes:** Zero figures should be entered in cells where appropriate).

Employee's weekly timesheet for week ending 21 July

Employee:	A. Lander		Profit centre:	Warehouse store man		
Employee number:	S007		Basic pay per hour:	£8.00		
	Total hours spent in work	Hours spent on indirect work	Notes	Basic pay £	Overtime premium £	Total pay £
Monday	8	½	Late delivery			
Tuesday	7½					
Wednesday	8	½	Early delivery			
Thursday	8	½	Cleaning warehouse			
Friday	7½					
Saturday	4		Stock taking			
Sunday	2		Stock taking			
Total	**45**	**1½**				

TASK 4 (18 MARKS)

Sarloue Ltd's budgeted overheads for the next financial year are:

	£	£
Depreciation of plant and equipment		135,000
Power for production machinery		17,500
Rent and rates		23,750
Light and heat		6,250
Indirect labour costs:		
Maintenance	10,000	
Stores	12,500	
Canteen	36,000	
Total indirect labour cost		58,500

The following information is also available:

Department	Carrying amount of plant and equipment	Production machinery power usage (KwH)	Floor space (square metres)	Number of employees
Production centres:				
Plastic moulding	180,000	22,500	2,000	20
Plastic extrusion	360,000	30,000	2,000	20
Support cost centres:				
Maintenance			1,000	2
Stores			3,000	2
Canteen			2,000	2
Total	540,000	52,500	10,000	46

Overheads are allocated or apportioned on the most appropriate basis. The total overheads of the support cost centres are then reapportioned on the follow bases:

- 60% of the Maintenance cost centre's time is spent maintaining production machinery in the Plastic moulding production centre and 30% of time is spent in the Plastic extrusion production centre. The remainder is spent maintaining the canteen equipment

- The Stores cost centre supports the two production centres equally

- The Canteen cost centre is reapportioned based on staff numbers in the two production centres only

Complete the overhead analysis table below:

	Basis of apportionment	Plastic moulding	Plastic extrusion	Maintenance	Stores	Canteen	Totals
Depreciation of plant and equipment							
Power for production machinery							
Rent and rates							
Light and heat							
Indirect labour							
Totals							
Reapportion Maintenance							
Reapportion Stores							
Reapportion Canteen							
Total overheads to production centres							

TASK 5 (15 MARKS)

Sarloue Ltd's budgeted overheads and activity levels are:

	Plastic moulding	Plastic extrusion
Budgeted overheads (£)	22,500	24,750
Budgeted direct labour hours	5,000	5,200
Budgeted machine hours	15,000	20,000

(a) **What would the budgeted overhead absorption rate for each department, if this were set based on being labour intensive, to the nearest penny?** **(4 marks)**

	Plastic moulding £	Plastic extrusion £
Budgeted overhead absorption rate	per hour	per hour

Additional data

At the end of the quarter actual overheads incurred were found to be:

	Plastic moulding £	Plastic extrusion £
Actual overheads	19,800	28,000

Overheads were recovered on a labour hour basis. The labour hours were 5% more than budgeted in Plastic moulding and 3% more in Plastic extrusion.

(b) **Calculate the overhead that was absorbed in each department and state the under or over absorption that occurred in each department (answers to the nearest £)** **(8 marks)**

	Actual hours worked	Absorbed amount £	Under/over	Value £
Plastic moulding				
Plastic extrusion				

Additional data

The overhead absorption rate in the plastic moulding department should have been based on machine hours. The actual machine hours for the period were 14,500 hours.

(c) **Complete the following table:** **(3 marks)**

	Overhead absorption rate £	Overhead absorbed £	Under/over absorption £
Plastics moulding department	per hour		Under/over

TASK 6 (25 MARKS)

Sarloue uses both batch and unit costing, as appropriate, in its plastic extrusion department. It is currently costing a new product LL45. LL45 will be produced in batches of 4,500.

It has been estimated that the following costs will be incurred in producing one batch of 4,500 units of LL45.

Product LL45	£
Direct materials £ per unit	6.00
Direct labour £ per unit	5.50
Variable overheads £ per batch	14,625
Total fixed manufacturing overheads	36,000
Total fixed administration, selling and distribution costs	19,170

(a) Calculate the estimated prime cost of per unit of LL45 (3 marks)

£

(b) Calculate the estimated marginal production cost of one batch of LL45 (3 marks)

£

(c) Calculate the estimated total full absorption cost of one batch of LL45: (3 marks)

£

(d) Calculate the estimated marginal cost per unit of LL45 (3 marks)

£

(e) Calculate the estimated full absorption cost per unit of LL45: (3 marks)

£

(f) A cost centre is defined as: (2 marks)

A   A unit of product or service for which costs are accumulated

B   A production or service location, function, activity or item of equipment for which costs are accumulated

C   Costs that relate directly to a unit

D   Costs that contain both a fixed and a variable element

(g) A manager is known as a profit centre manager, which of the following does the manager control?   (3 marks)

A   Departmental variable costs

B   Departmental total costs

C   Departmental total costs and revenues

D   Departmental total costs, revenues, assets and liabilities

(h) Why might Sarloue decide to allocate its costs between the products of different departments?   (3 marks)

A   To reduce its overall inventory valuation

B   To comply with accounting standards

C   To report segmented profits/losses

D   To speed up its internal reporting

(i) Which of these is an example of unethical behaviour by an accounting technician?   (2 marks)

A   Treating costs as confidential

B   Calculating profits subjectively rather than objectively

C   Valuing inventory in a consistent manner period to period

D   Allocating costs between products objectively

TASK 7 (16 MARKS)

Sarloue has a contract with a customer to produce 5,000 litres of GG99. Revenues and costs for 5,000 litres are shown below.

Possible production level	5,000 litres
	£
Sales revenue	145,000
Variable and semi-variable costs:	
Material	30,000
Labour	40,000
Overheads	25,000
Fixed costs:	
Indirect labour	20,000
Overheads	15,000
Target profit for contract	11,500

The labour cost is a semi-variable cost. The fixed cost is £20,000 and the variable cost is £4.00 per unit.

Use the table below to calculate the required number of units for this contract to achieve its target profit. Enter the contribution per mile to two decimal places.

Calculation of required number of litres	£
Fixed costs	
Target profit	
Fixed cost and target profit	
Sales revenue	
Variable costs	
Contribution	
Contribution per unit	
Required number of litres to achieve target profit	

TASK 8 (16 MARKS)

Sarloue Ltd has prepared a forecast for the next quarter for three of its engineered components, GG57, HH23 and KK12.

The company expects to produce and sell 1,000 GG57 and 1,500 HH23. The budgeted sales demand for KK12 is 25% greater than that of HH23. Budgeted total fixed costs are £12,750

Other budgeted information for the three products is as follows:

Product	GG57	HH23	KK12
Sales revenue (£)	25,000	20,625	20,625
Direct materials (£)	7,500	7,870	5,622
Direct labour (£)	8,750	6,000	3,750
Variable overheads (£)	4,500	3,500	4,120

Complete the table below (to TWO decimal places) to show the budgeted contribution per unit of product sold.

	GG57 (£)	HH23 (£)	KK12 (£)	Total (£)
Selling price per unit				
Less: variable costs per unit:				
Direct materials				
Direct labour				
Variable overheads				
Contribution per unit				
Sales volume (units)				
Total contribution				
Less: fixed cost				
Budgeted profit/loss				

TASK 9   **(16 MARKS)**

Sarloue Ltd has the following original budget and actual performance for product GG101 for the year ending 31 December.

	Budget	*Actual*
Volume sold	20,000	18,500
Sales revenue	40,000	38,850
Less costs:		
Direct materials	16,000	17,575
Direct labour	10,000	10,175
Overheads	2,000	1,950
Operating profit	12,000	9,150

Both direct materials and direct labour are variable costs, but the overheads are fixed.

(a)   Complete the table below to show a flexed budget and the resulting variances against this budget for the year. Show the actual variance amount, for sales and each cost, in the column headed 'Variance'   **(12 marks)**

Note

- **Adverse variances must be denoted with a minus sign or bracket**
- **Enter 0 where any figure is zero**

	Flexed budget	*Actual*	*Variance*
Volume sold		18,500	
Sales revenue		38,850	
Less costs:			
Direct materials		17,575	
Direct labour		10,175	
Overheads		1,950	
Profit from operations		9,150	

(b)   Referring to your answer for part (a), which one of the following has had the greatest impact in decreasing the profit from operations?   **(2 mark)**

A   Sales revenue

B   Direct materials

C   Direct labour

D   Variable overheads

(c)   Which of the following might have caused the variance for direct labour?   **(2 mark)**

A   An increase in units produced

B   An decrease in employees' pay

C   Improved efficiency of employees

D   An increase in overtime

TASK 10 (20 MARKS)

One of the extrusion machines in the Plastic extrusion department is nearing the end of its useful life and Sarloue Ltd is considering purchasing a replacement machine.

Estimates have been made for the initial capital cost, sales income and operating costs of the replacement machine, which is expected to have a useful life of three years:

	Year 0 £000	Year 1 £000	Year 2 £000	Year 3 £000
Capital expenditure	450			
Other cash flows:				
Sales income		600	650	750
Operating costs		420	480	510

The company appraises capital investment projects using a 15% cost of capital.

(a) Complete the table below and calculate the net present value of the proposed replacement machine (to the nearest £000). (14 marks)

	Year 0 £000	Year 1 £000	Year 2 £000	Year 3 £000
Capital expenditure				
Sales income				
Operating costs				
Net cash flows				
PV factors	1.0000	0.8696	0.7561	0.6575
Discounted cash flows				
Net present value				

The net present value is *positive/negative**

*delete as appropriate

(b) The IRR for this project will be *greater than/less than** 15% (2 marks)

(c) Calculate the payback of the proposed replacement machine to the nearest whole month. (4 marks)

The payback period is _____Year(s) and _____Months

Section 4

ANSWERS TO MOCK ASSESSMENT QUESTIONS

TASK 1

	Cost (£)
AVCO issue	1,376
AVCO balance	2,944
FIFO issue	1,320
FIFO balance	3,000

TASK 2

	Account	Dr (£)	Cr (£)
Transaction 1	Inventory	1,820	
	Bank		1,820
Transaction 2	Production	1,080	
	Inventory		1,080
Transaction 3	Inventory	1,410	
	Trade payables' control		1,410
Transaction 4	Trade payables' control	1,500	
	Inventory		1,500

TASK 3

Employee's weekly timesheet for week ending 21 July

Employee:	A. Lander		Profit centre:		Warehouse store man	
Employee number:	S007		Basic pay per hour:		£8.00	
	Total hours spent in work	*Hours spent on indirect work*	*Notes*	*Basic pay £*	*Overtime premium £*	*Total pay £*
Monday	8	½	Late delivery	64	2	66
Tuesday	7½			60	0	60
Wednesday	8	½	Early delivery	64	2	66
Thursday	8	½	Cleaning warehouse	64	2	66
Friday	7½			60	0	60
Saturday	4		Stock taking	32	32	64
Sunday*	2		Stock taking	16	16	32
Total	**37**	**1½**		360	54	414

* Alternative answer for Sunday

Sunday*	2		Stock taking	0	32	32
Total	**37**	**1½**		344	70	414

TASK 4

	Basis of apportionment	Plastic moulding £	Plastic extrusion £	Maintenance £	Stores £	Canteen £	Totals £
Depreciation of plant and equipment	CA of plant and equipment	45,000	90,000	0	0	0	135,000
Power for production machinery	Production machinery power usage (KwH)	7,500	10,000	0	0	0	17,500
Rent and rates	Floor space	4,750	4,750	2,375	7,125	4,750	23,750
Light and heat	Floor space	1,250	1,250	625	1,875	1,250	6,250
Indirect labour	Allocated	0	0	10,000	12,500	36,000	58,500
Totals		**58,500**	**106,000**	**13,000**	**21,500**	**42,000**	**241,000**
Reapportion Maintenance		7,800	3,900	(13,000)		1,300	
Reapportion Stores		10,750	10,750		(21,500)		
Reapportion Canteen		21,650	21,650			(43,300)	
Total overheads to production centres		98,700	142,300				241,000

TASK 5

(a)

	Plastic moulding £	Plastic extrusion £
Budgeted overhead absorption rate	4.50 per hour	4.76 per hour

Plastic moulding = 22,500 ÷ 5,000 = £4.50 and Plastic extrusion = 24,750 ÷ 5,200 = £4.76.

(b)

	Actual hours worked	Absorbed amount £	Under/over	Value £
Plastic moulding	5,000 × 1.05 = 5,250	£4.50 × 5,250 = £23,625	Over	£23,625 − £19,800 = £3,825
Plastic extrusion	5,200 × 1.03 = 5,356	£4.76 × 5,356 = £25,495	Under	£28,000 − £25,495 = £2,505

(c)

	Overhead absorption rate £	Overhead absorbed £	Under/over absorption £
Plastics moulding department	22,500 ÷ 15,000 = 1.50 per hour	1.50 × 14,500 = 21,750	21,750 − 19,800 = 1,950 over

TASK 6

(a) £6.00 + £5.50 = £11.50

(b) (£11.50 × 4,500) + £14,625 = £66,375

(c) £66,375 + £36,000 = £102,375

(d) £66,375 ÷ 4,500 = £14.75

(e) £102,375 ÷ 4,500 = £22.75

(f) B

(g) C

(h) C

(i) B

TASK 7

Calculation of required number of litres	£
Fixed costs	55,000
Target profit	11,500
Fixed cost and target profit	66,500
Sales revenue	145,000
Variable costs	75,000
Contribution	70,000
Contribution per unit	14
Required number of litres to achieve target profit	4,750

TASK 8

	GG57 (£)	HH23 (£)	KK12 (£)	Total (£)
Selling price per unit	25.00	13.75	11.00	
Less: variable costs per unit:				
• Direct materials	7.50	5.25	3.00	
• Direct labour	8.75	4.00	2.00	
• Variable overheads	4.50	2.33	2.20	
Contribution per unit	4.25	2.17	3.80	
Sales volume (units)	1,000	1,500	1,875	
Total contribution	4,250	3,255	7,125	14,630
Less: fixed cost				12,750
Budgeted profit/loss				1,880

TASK 9

(a)

	Flexed budget	Actual	Variance
Volume sold	18,500	18,500	
Sales revenue	37,000	38,850	1,850
Less costs:			
Direct materials	14,800	17,575	−2,775
Direct labour	9,250	10,175	−925
Overheads	2,000	1,950	50
Operating profit	10,950	9,150	−1,800

(b) B

(c) D

TASK 10

(a)

	Year 0 £000	Year 1 £000	Year 2 £000	Year 3 £000
Capital expenditure	(450)			
Sales income		600	650	750
Operating costs		(420)	(480)	(510)
Net cash flows	(450)	180	170	240
PV factors	1.0000	0.8696	0.7561	0.6575
Discounted cash flows	(450)	157	129	158
Net present value	(6)			

The net present value is **negative**

(b)   The IRR for this project will be **less than** 15%

(c)

Year	Cash flow £000	Cumulative cash flow £000
0	(450)	(450)
1	180	(270)
2	170	(100)
3	240	140

The payback period is **2** years and **5** months. Months = 100/240 × 12 = 5 months